W9-AXQ-842

TRUE FOOD

TRUE FOOD

Seasonal, Sustainable, Simple, Pure

Andrew Weil, MD, and Sam Fox,
with Michael Stebner

PHOTOGRAPHS BY DITTE ISAGER

LB

LITTLE, BROWN AND COMPANY
NEW YORK   BOSTON   LONDON

Also by Andrew Weil, MD

Spontaneous Happiness: A New Path to Emotional Well-Being

You Can't Afford to Get Sick: Your Guide to Optimum Health and Health Care
(originally published as *Why Our Health Matters*)

Integrative Oncology
(with Donald Abrams, MD)

Healthy Aging: A Lifelong Guide to Your Well-Being

The Healthy Kitchen: Recipes for a Better Body, Life, and Spirit
(with Rosie Daley)

*Eating Well for Optimum Health: The Essential Guide
to Food, Diet, and Nutrition*

*Eight Weeks to Optimum Health: A Proven Program for Taking Advantage
of Your Body's Natural Healing Power*

*Spontaneous Healing: How to Discover and Enhance
Your Body's Natural Ability to Maintain and Heal Itself*

*Natural Health, Natural Medicine: The Complete Guide to Wellness and
Self-Care for Optimum Health*

Health and Healing

From Chocolate to Morphine: Everything You Need to Know About Mind-Altering Drugs
(with Winifred Rosen)

*The Marriage of the Sun and Moon: Dispatches from
the Frontiers of Consciousness*

The Natural Mind: A Revolutionary Approach to the Drug Problem

For all lovers of True Food

Copyright © 2012 by Andrew Weil, MD

All rights reserved. In accordance with the U.S. Copyright Act of 1976, the scanning, uploading, and electronic sharing of any part of this book without the permission of the publisher constitute unlawful piracy and theft of the author's intellectual property. If you would like to use material from the book (other than for review purposes), prior written permission must be obtained by contacting the publisher at permissions@hbgusa.com. Thank you for your support of the author's rights.

Little, Brown and Company
Hachette Book Group
1290 Avenue of the Americas, New York, NY 10104
littlebrown.com

Originally published in hardcover by Little, Brown and Company, October 2012
First paperback edition, April 2014

Little, Brown and Company is a division of Hachette Book Group, Inc. The Little, Brown name and logo are trademarks of Hachette Book Group, Inc.

The publisher is not responsible for websites (or their content) that are not owned by the publisher.

ISBN 978-0-316-12941-1 (hc) / 978-0-316-12940-4 (pb)
LCCN 2012939982

10 9 8 7 6 5 4 3

IM

Book and jacket design by Gary Tooth / Empire Design Studio

Printed in China

Contents

Introduction: The Doctor, the Chef, and the Restaurateur

Over cold sake and edamame, Andrew Weil, MD, shared his food history and philosophy with Michael Stebner, executive chef of True Food Kitchen, and Sam Fox, CEO of Fox Restaurant Concepts.

ANDREW WEIL: A lot of people ask me how I got into the restaurant business.

MICHAEL STEBNER: Do you tell them it was an honest mistake?

SAM FOX: We all screw up. Don't be too hard on yourself.

AW: Actually, for years, people I've cooked for have urged me to open a restaurant, and I always felt it would be too risky. I've long been a good cook, but I knew nothing about the restaurant business. And I had enough to do without adding running a restaurant to my bucket list.

SF: When did you start cooking?

AW: I did some with my grandmother when I was a kid in Philadelphia, but I only really started when I was on my own as a medical student in Boston. Hospital food was awful, and I found that envisioning a great meal, then creating it, was just what I needed to decompress after a long shift. At first I followed recipes but soon found that I was good at inventing dishes. When I was 17, I took a year off between high school and college to travel the world, and came back to the U.S. with a whole new appreciation for food, especially Asian and Mediterranean dishes. In the 1970s, I spent a lot of time knocking around in Latin America and Africa researching—and eating!— exotic fruits and vegetables and learning a lot more about traditional foods. All of this has gone into my food philosophy.

MS: For me, I always figured I'd be in the auto repair business like my father, but in 1989, when I was 16, I got a job as a busboy at the Radisson Hotel, in Phoenix. That first day, it just clicked. I camped out in the kitchen and talked the chef into letting me train with him. He was really kind and generous and took me under his wing.

SF: That's how it was done back then. It was better in some ways.

MS: There wasn't a culinary school on every corner. You learned on the job, which had some real advantages. Your resume wasn't a piece of paper; it was what you could cook and serve. I started working at the Phoenician when I was 20, which at that time—1993—was the most advanced kitchen in Phoenix. The chef there, James Boyce, saw something in me and gave me a chance to work at a very high level for 18 months. After that, with a few detours, I worked in better and better restaurants, including Region, which I owned and ran in San Diego.

AW: And Sam, you've been in it your whole life?

SF: Seems like more than one life, sometimes. I'm a third-generation retail-food guy. I grew up in my grandparents' and parents' restaurants. Did my homework in a booth. My folks always had mom-and-pop-type restaurants in Tucson, never more than one at a time: a Jewish deli, a Mexican restaurant, a place called the Hungry Fox. The restaurant business was by no means hip—it was a grind,

16 hours a day, sometimes seven days a week, money always tight, a life sentence without parole. My mom and pop tried hard to get me out of it. So I went to the University of Arizona to learn real estate finance. I was interning at a real estate firm, and I really thought I was on another path.

AW: So what happened?

SF: In July 1988, the guy I was interning for told me to go to his house and help his wife—she'd had a flat tire. I spent 45 minutes changing it, getting grease all over my new khakis, broiling; it was probably 140 degrees on that concrete. I'd never been so aggravated—this was learning the real estate business?—and patience has never been my strong suit. I drove back to the office, quit, and made a solemn vow at the age of 20: I would never, ever work for anyone else. I'm just not built for it.

I dropped out of school and opened a restaurant in Tucson called Gilligan's, using $40,000 in borrowed money. It was insane. I was 20 years old and knew nothing about the business side of restaurants: payroll, taxes, nothing, not one thing, could not even balance my checkbook. I didn't really know cooking, either. About a month into it, my chef and I got in a fight. He threw a punch at me, I ducked, and he hit the brick wall and shattered his hand. For the next six months, he sat on a barstool and taught me how to cook. So that was my culinary school.

AW: Good thing you could duck.

SF: It's come in handy more than once. Anyway, to make a long story very short, I got a partner and we started to open one place after another in Tucson, then in Phoenix. I think the main reason my places succeed is that I try to provide a total experience. I do the interior design, I sample all the food, I take every accumulated scrap of knowledge I have as a result of marinating in this business for my whole life and apply it every day.

AW: As you were going deeper into the restaurant business, I was getting farther away—I wasn't even involved as a customer. Increasingly, I found that restaurant menus simply didn't offer much that I found both healthy and appealing. Usually, I felt I could make better food at home. My own cooking evolved toward simpler dishes with bold flavors.

Since my dinner guests—a pretty varied lot—always loved my food, it seemed to me that these dishes could work in a restaurant. So when Richard [Richard Baxter, Dr. Weil's business partner] introduced me to you in 2007, I told you I'd love to see a new concept: a restaurant that would offer delicious food that is also good for you. Until then, no one had successfully brought together the worlds of fine dining and healthy eating. But you were less than enthusiastic.

SF: That's because health food doesn't sell.

AW: Right. The "health food" restaurants I knew served food that's boring, weird, or both. I tried to make it clear to you that I wasn't talking about tofu and sprouts.

SF: I wasn't convinced. When I thought of Andy Weil, I thought: hippie, Birkenstocks, vegan food. That wasn't how I ate or lived. So I stalled, but finally, Richard called me up and said, "You need to try Andy's food. Come to his ranch." So my wife and I went. You lived way, way out at the end of a very bad road about 10 miles southeast of Tucson. Heading out there in the dark, wondering if my muffler would shake off, I had no idea what to expect. I knew you only by reputation, and you really didn't know

me at all. But as it turned out, it was a great time: We talked, you showed us around this spectacular 1920s house and property where you lived, and we had an amazing meal.

AW: I made curried cauliflower soup, a vegetarian Caesar salad, salmon cakes, and a nondairy frozen dessert with cashew milk. After dinner, you seemed a little more open to the concept.

SF: I was. It was a killer meal, and it started to dawn on me that this was the future. It seemed that every day in our restaurants, we were getting more requests for vegetarian, vegan, gluten-free, all of that. Maybe, after three decades of eating crap that made them fatter and sicker, people really would factor health into their restaurant choices—if the food were good!

So I found a location in Phoenix that would be ideal, a coffee shop that was closing in Biltmore Fashion Park. We formed a partnership, and I came up with a name: True Food Kitchen.

AW: So now we had to get serious.

SF: Right. The main thing would be finding a chef who could translate the concept into the reality of a restaurant. And I had the right guy.

MS: I was the executive chef at Greene House in Scottsdale when you approached me about a partnership with Dr. Weil. I knew about Andy and was very interested in everything he was doing. We set up a first meeting, and I drove the dirt road in the middle of the desert to his ranch house. The minute Andy and I started talking, we both knew it was the right thing.

AW: Absolutely.

MS: I could see you had a passion for food and an almost fanatical respect for the quality of ingredients and the integrity of traditional, simple dishes. It was never, "Let's see if we can make a healthy version of shepherd's pie." It was, "Let's adapt this dish from Tokyo or Bangkok or northern Italy, make a few small tweaks in line with what's fresh in the local market, and see what we get." While I had the technique, you had this amazing, encyclopedic knowledge of dishes and ingredients.

AW: Based on 50 years of traveling and study—you do pick up a few things!

MS: You introduced me to olivello (sea buckthorn) juice, tempeh, hemp seeds, the list goes on. I loved them all. There is nothing more exciting to me than finding a way to use a new ingredient, a new flavor. It reminded me of being in my mother's kitchen as a kid growing up in Oregon. That's just joyous to me.

AW: I knew you were the man for the job when I gave you some olivello juice in sparkling water with a touch of agave nectar and asked how you would use it in a sorbet. In minutes, you came up with a recipe, using fresh orange juice and a vanilla bean. The balance of flavors was perfect, on the first try. Orange and Sea Buckthorn Sorbet is now a major hit at all TFK locations [you'll find the recipe on page 216]. Over the next few weeks, we traded ideas and recipes nonstop.

MS: And I got a crash course in the Anti-Inflammatory Diet. So I spent basically the whole summer of 2008 in the Fox Restaurant Concepts test kitchen in Phoenix, creating the True Food Kitchen menu, tweaking ideas that you e-mailed me every day from your summer house. I'm a classically trained French chef, and the biggest revelation to me while working with you was the Asian flavors, especially the various aspects of umami, the "fifth taste." I'm still exploring that one.

SF: As the opening got closer, I still thought a lot of the recipes and ingredients might be too weird for a mainstream clientele. I wanted steak tacos on the menu; Andy wanted mostly fish and veggies with just a few chicken and turkey dishes. I don't like spicy food. I don't like olives. I don't think many people do.

AW: I love chiles, and I've almost never met an olive I didn't like.

SF: The idea of kale pesto seemed too much like eating grass.

AW: Yes, but you tried to "fix" it by diluting it with an oily garlic sauce that turned it a muddy yellow-green, lowered its nutritional value, and ruined the flavor.

SF: That's debatable, but I definitely couldn't stand that banana-coconut black rice pudding thing.

AW: Which is a very popular street food in Thailand, and a huge hit whenever I make it for my dinner guests. [The recipe is on page 212, and I'm still trying to get it on the True Food Kitchen menu.] Anyway, I've since learned that many of your instincts are right. The steak tacos were an instant bestseller when the Phoenix restaurant opened.

SF: When you said the artificial sweeteners on the tables had to go, it seemed nuts—you have got to have those.

AW: But as I told you, erythritol is better. It's a safe, natural, noncaloric sweetener. That's what we offer now, along with a stevia-based sweetener. I also held my ground in keeping conventional commercially farmed salmon off the menu.

And when organic black kale was in short supply and crazy expensive, I refused to let the kitchen substitute conventionally grown product.

SF: When I found out that kale is on the Environmental Working Group's "Dirty Dozen" list of crops with the highest pesticide residues, I went along.

AW: With each opening, it's getting easier to work together. We better understand each other's points of view. You've made me aware of the practical realities of transforming the ideas of a home cook into a successful restaurant. I respect your dedication, and your instinct for selecting the outstanding managers you've put in charge of each True Food Kitchen. The professionalism of your company is exemplary.

So despite the fights, or maybe because of them, True Food Kitchen was an immediate, runaway success.

MS: We opened the Biltmore location in Phoenix in October of 2008—in the teeth of the recession—and lines have snaked out the door there and at the other locations ever since. Pretty clearly, the public was ready for this.

SF: Almost immediately, we noticed something that's very rare in the restaurant business: people eating here three, four, five nights a week. If you eat that often in most American restaurants, you will suffer—portions are so huge these days, and the ingredients are the cheapest possible. One of the coolest things is that professional athletes in town discovered us early: Grant Hill and Steve Nash of the Phoenix Suns are in here all the time. So the world needed this more than I had realized.

As it turned out, I needed it, too. In February 2010, I woke up in the night with bad chest pains. I went to the hospital and they found a blockage in one of my coronary arteries. It was probably caused by diet as much as anything. I was in serious danger of dropping dead at age 42. I got a stent inserted, and I had a wake-up call: I need to eat at True Food Kitchen more often and start living the whole Andy Weil lifestyle. So now it's like my therapy. I probably still work too hard and need to meditate and do some other Weil-y things, but at least, if I start to feel bad, I make a point of eating at True Food three days in a row. It feels like it gets me back on track.

MS: To me, the walk-in cooler tells the whole story. We have these vast shelves of veggies and tiny ones for meat and dairy. I love to show it to professional chefs; their mouths drop open, it just looks backward to them. But that ratio is reflected in every serving. We may put 9 ounces of veggies, 4 ounces of starch, and 5 ounces of animal protein on your plate. Other restaurants would reverse those numbers—13 ounces of meat and just 5 ounces of plant-based foods. And carbs and starches play a small role—at the moment, we use potatoes in just one dish, and we serve our own pita bread with an herbed hummus appetizer. It is the only table bread we serve.

Staff training at True Food is intense. The customers who are gluten intolerant, vegan, or diabetic—and there are a lot of them—ask about everything: How much fat? How many carbs? Is it really gluten-free? And so on. The staff has to be educated and sharp, and they are certainly motivated. We have servers who have nutrition degrees, or who have taught yoga for years, who can draw on a deep well of knowledge. It's definitely not your usual restaurant crew. We do far more training and hold far more staff tastings than the average restaurant. People are really proud to be part of this, and the word has gotten out. When we

have job fairs to open new locations, there is a line out the door. Getting good staff has never been a problem.

AW: I'm proud, too. I'm thrilled to be able to introduce people to food that tastes great because it's made with the best and freshest ingredients. It's simple. It's skillfully prepared. It conforms to a nutritional philosophy consistent with the best available scientific evidence.

The greatest challenge I've faced since the 1970s in trying to change American eating habits for the better is the widely held belief that food that tastes good and food that promotes health are in opposition—it's either/or, but it can't be both/and. The only way I know to convince people otherwise is to give them the experience of food that is both good and good for you. I've tried in the past to do that by putting recipes out there—in books, in articles, on my website, and in my social media. Now, with the restaurants, I can do it much more efficiently. I am just overjoyed by the popularity of True Food. I believe it will help propel a food revolution that's taking place throughout the country.

MS: Yes, it's a good time to take good food seriously.

AW: And I've been delighted to find that it's never too late to realize a dream. I was 66 years old when our first location opened. I've found mulling over potential locations, or diving into the intricacies of a new Thai dish, to be far more engaging than any retirement plan I could have dreamed up. So I guess that would be my last observation to put out to the world: If you've nurtured an idea for a long time, I assure you that the decades you've spent incubating it will prove to be a blessing, not a burden. The perspective and maturity you can bring to a project after a lifetime of real-world experiences can be great assets.

Just be sure you get plenty of help.

The True Food Pantry

At True Food Kitchen, we use ingredients that may be unfamiliar to some. Most of them, however, may be purchased in supermarkets, at Asian groceries, or online.

AGAVE NECTAR: Also known as *agave syrup,* this sweetener comes from the same plant from which tequila is made. Available in supermarkets, agave has a texture similar to honey and a neutral flavor, and it dissolves quickly. Use $\frac{1}{3}$ cup agave nectar for every 1 cup sugar. Store in an airtight container in a cool, dry place.

ASTRAGALUS ROOT: The sliced, dried root of *Astragalus membranaceous* is a common medicinal ingredient in Chinese cuisine. It is available at Chinese herb stores and online, and the slices are in fairly standard sizes of 5 to 8 inches long. Simmered in soups, it adds a pleasant, sweet flavor. It also increases resistance to colds and flu and boosts immunity. Remove the root slices before serving.

BALSAMIC VINEGAR: True balsamic vinegar is made from a reduction of pressed Trebbiano grapes in northern Italy, around the town of Modena. The resulting thick syrup is then aged for a minimum of 12 years. Balsamic vinegar's flavor is a balance of sour and sweet. It gains much of its flavor from the series of different wooden casks in which it is aged. The best, and most costly, balsamic vinegar (found in Italy or in specialty shops and online) is labeled *aceto balsamico tradizionale.* Commercially manufactured balsamic vinegars that are widely found in supermarkets are made from grape juice, sweeteners, and coloring. Legally these cheaper variations can't be called *traditional* or *tradizionale,* even if they still say "Aceto Balsamico di Modena" on the label. These less expensive versions are suitable for marinades, vinaigrettes, and pan sauces. Once opened, store capped tightly in a cool, dry place, such as a cupboard.

CHILES: We use a lot of fresh chiles at True Food. How much and which varieties you use are entirely up to you. The general rule is that the smaller the chile, the hotter it is. And most of the heat comes from the white membranes that attach to the seeds. Among our favorites:

Anaheim chiles are light green and mild; they should be roasted before they are used in cooking.

Arbol are slender, fiery chiles that turn from green to red as they ripen. Use judiciously.

Fresnos are small, conical-shaped peppers that look like jalapeños, except that they mature from green to orange to red (becoming hotter as they mature).

Jalapeños are harvested when still green and usually sold that way. When jalapeños are dried and smoked, they are called *chipotles.*

Dark green poblanos are larger and less hot than many other chiles. Similar in color and shape to green bell peppers, the poblano is slightly elongated at the bottom tip. Because of its fairly mild flavor and large size, the poblano is often stuffed and baked.

Choose peppers that are free of blemishes or dark spots and whose skin is taut. Stored in a paper bag in the vegetable compartment of the refrigerator, they should last for up to a week.

CHINESE BLACK VINEGAR: Brewed from mixed grains, this vinegar has a complex, fruity flavor that is reminiscent of Worcestershire sauce. Brands from the city of Chingkiang (Zhenjiang) are superior. Chinese black vinegar is available at Asian food stores and online.

EVAPORATED CANE SUGAR: Evaporated cane sugar is made from fresh sugarcane juice that is evaporated and then crystallized. It has a bit of color and flavor from trace minerals, which are removed with further refining to white sugar. It should be stored in an airtight container in a cool, dry place.

EXPELLER-PRESSED CANOLA OIL: This oil is mechanically pressed from the canola seed (also known as rapeseed). In traditional canola oils, the oil is extracted from the seeds using heat and chemical solvents, which damage the fatty acids. Only gentle pressure is used in expeller pressing. Buy organic brands. Canola oil has a relatively high smoke point (but never heat it anywhere near that), and it provides some omega-3 fatty acids.

FLAX MEAL: It's best to make this yourself, as it goes rancid quickly upon exposure to air. Buy organic flax seeds—either light or dark ones—and grind them in a small electric coffee grinder that you just use for flax. Make just enough to last you for a few days and store any unused meal in a tightly sealed container in the refrigerator.

GARAM MASALA: The ingredients in this mixture of ground spices commonly used in Indian cooking vary regionally but often include black pepper, cumin, coriander, cardamom, and cinnamon. Buy it in Asian stores or make your own, using recipes you can find online. Store in an airtight container.

GINGER: Purchase fresh ginger that is plump and firm. The easiest way to get the most flavor from ginger is to peel off the skin with a vegetable peeler, then use a Microplane grater or rasp to grate the ginger along its length.

JICAMA: A large, light brown root that looks like a turnip (although unrelated—it's a cousin to the sweet potato), jicama has a crisp, sweet texture. It is popular in Mexican cooking and is often eaten raw in salads. The tough peel must be removed—just eat the white flesh. Look for jicama roots that are dry and round and no bigger than the size of two fists; larger ones may be too starchy. Refrigerate jicama for up to two weeks.

KAFFIR LIME LEAVES: The leaves of the kaffir lime tree are often called for in Southeast Asian recipes, including soups and curries. The leaf is typically used whole, like a bay leaf, and removed before serving. Look for them fresh in Asian markets and some gourmet food shops, or online at importfood.com. Store the leaves in resealable bags in the freezer for several months. Zest of regular limes may be substituted.

LIGHT COCONUT MILK: Coconut milk is made by shredding and soaking white coconut flesh in warm water and then pressing out much of the liquid. Light coconut milk comes from the second pressing of the coconut flesh. It is simply less concentrated, lower in fat, and lighter in flavor. An important ingredient in Thai recipes, coconut milk and light coconut milk are easily found canned in most supermarkets in the ethnic food aisle. After opening, any extra may be stored in a lidded container in the refrigerator for just a few days. (It spoils quickly.)

MARCONA ALMONDS: This variety of almond from Spain is rounder, softer, and sweeter than California almonds. Marcona almonds can be found in most natural foods stores and supermarkets, as well as at gourmet food shops and online. Because of their high oil content, buy only what you need, storing the rest in an airtight container in a cool, dry place or in the freezer.

MIRIN: This rice wine is similar to sake, except that mirin is sweet (containing between 40 and 50 percent sugar). It is used as a condiment, often in place of sugar in Japan. For the best flavor, look for mirin labeled *hon-mirin: honjozo* (which means "true mirin: naturally brewed") as opposed to commercial brands, which are mostly high-fructose corn syrup. Mirin can be found in Asian markets. Once opened, it will retain its flavor, stored in the refrigerator, for two months.

NUTRITIONAL YEAST FLAKES: This inactive yeast has a nutty, cheese-like flavor. It is a source of B-complex vitamins, is high in folic acid, is gluten-free, and is a complete protein. Because of this and its savory flavor, it is useful and popular in vegan diets. Choose yeast flakes over granules, as flakes have a smoother texture and better taste. You can purchase nutritional yeast flakes in health food stores, in the bulk food section. Store in an airtight container in a cool, dry place, such as a cupboard.

RICE WINE VINEGAR: Important in Japanese, Chinese, Vietnamese, and Korean cuisines, rice wine vinegar can be made from white, red, or black rice. Its flavor is mellower and sweeter than that of Western-style vinegars. Rice wine vinegar comes seasoned or unseasoned; we prefer the latter. Store capped tightly in a cool, dry place; it keeps for at least three months.

SAMBAL OELEK: This spicy paste of Malaysian and Indonesian origin has the pure taste of chiles with little else and is used more in cooking than as a condiment. It is available at Asian food stores and online. Once opened, the jar should be kept in the refrigerator and the "best by" date should be observed.

SAN MARZANO TOMATOES: With the name describing both a point of origin and a variety of tomato, the San Marzano looks similar to a plum tomato, only slightly thinner and longer, with meatier flesh and fewer seeds. Harvested by hand, the tomatoes have a sweet, less acidic flavor that makes them prized both in Italy and around the world. When buying a can of San Marzanos, look for the D.O.P. seal (*Denominazione di Origine Protetta,* meaning "Protected Designation of Origin") to ensure authenticity. Store in a cool, dry place until opening. Keep any unused tomatoes in an airtight container in the refrigerator for up to three days.

SEA BUCKTHORN: The small orange fruit of this spiny shrub (*Hippophae rhamnoides*), native to Europe and Asia and also known as *olivello,* is rich in antioxidants. Sea buckthorn juice is available in some natural foods stores and online.

SPELT FLOUR: Spelt is a species of wheat cultivated in Europe since antiquity, now having renewed popularity as a tastier alternative to common wheat. Although it contains a moderate amount of gluten, spelt is tolerated by some people with wheat allergies or sensitivities. You can find spelt flour at most natural foods stores and online.

SRIRACHA: This type of Thai hot sauce is made from chile paste, vinegar, sugar, garlic, and salt. Look for brands with only those ingredients in larger supermarkets and Asian food stores or online.

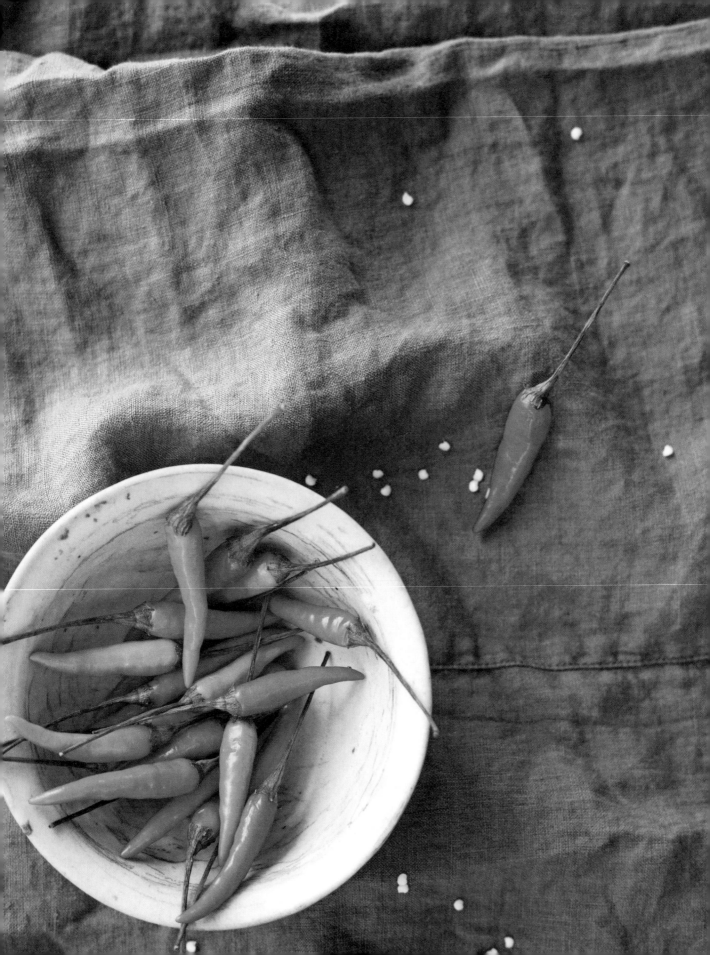

TAHINI: This paste made from ground sesame seeds is used in the cuisines of Asia, the Middle East, North Africa, Greece/Cyprus, and Turkey. It is an important component in hummus. Tahini can widely be found jarred or canned, in supermarkets as well as in gourmet and ethnic food shops. Buy raw tahini only. Once opened, store tahini in the refrigerator.

TAMARI: Like soy sauce, tamari is made from fermented soybeans, but it has a deeper, more complex flavor than many commercial soy sauces. Tamari is wheat-free, making it ideal for those who are gluten intolerant, whereas soy sauce is often made with wheat or other grains.

VEGETARIAN WORCESTERSHIRE SAUCE: A fermented liquid condiment with origins in Worcester, England, the sauce was first brought to market by John Lea and William Perrins in 1837. The difference between traditional Worcestershire sauce and vegetarian Worcestershire sauce is that the original sauce contains anchovies and the vegetarian version does not. Once opened, store vegetarian Worcestershire sauce in the refrigerator for up to two years.

WHITE BALSAMIC VINEGAR: Made in the same manner as traditional dark balsamic vinegar, white balsamic vinegar is made from white wine vinegar and pressed grape juice with seeds and skins. It is cooked, often under pressure to reduce potential caramelization and coloration. The flavor is similar to balsamic vinegar, if not slightly milder. Useful for aesthetic reasons, it is also less likely to overpower the more subtle flavors in a dish. Store capped tightly in a cool, dry place.

WHITE MISO: Miso is a Japanese seasoning paste made by fermenting soybeans, with or without the addition of grains like rice or barley or vegetables and spices. Common varieties of plain miso in addition to white (*shiromiso*) are red (*akamiso*) and mixed (*awasemiso*). You will find them in sealed containers in the refrigerated sections of Asian grocery stores and gourmet and health food shops. Refrigerated miso keeps indefinitely.

YUZU JUICE: Made from the yuzu citrus fruit, this juice has a sour flavor, often described as a cross between lime and grapefruit. It's more potent than lemon juice and should be used judiciously. Yuzu juice plays an important role in authentic Japanese and Korean cuisines; it is an ingredient in Japanese ponzu sauce. Freshly squeezed yuzu juice is hard to find in North America, but bottled juice is sold in Asian stores, gourmet shops, and online. Store according to the bottle's directions.

YUZU KOSHO: This is a thick, spicy Japanese paste made from the zest of yuzu fruit, red or green chile peppers, and salt. Use this condiment, available at Asian stores and online, in sauces or in rubs for fish and chicken. Store in the refrigerator.

BREAKFAST

I believe in starting the day with a satisfying breakfast, but I've never cared much for standard American morning foods. I love the traditional Japanese breakfast of miso soup, broiled salmon, steamed rice, pickled vegetables, seaweed, and green tea. At home I might have a slice of whole-grain rye bread with cheese or baked pressed tofu or Greek yogurt with olive oil, olives, and raw vegetables. On the road I have a harder time. But the True Food Kitchen brunch menu gives me plenty of options, and the recipes that follow are varied enough to suit many tastes. My personal favorite is the Crustless Quiche with Smoked Sable and Caraway Tofu (page 25). AW

Morning Glory

Weekend Warrior

Morning Glory

The modern smoothie has become sophisticated, often featuring exotic fruits. This one returns to 1970s-era smoothie essentials with its strawberry-banana base, but it gets an update from coconut milk and agave nectar. We make it seasonally using only fresh strawberries. AW

1	banana
8	strawberries
2	tablespoons coconut milk
2	teaspoons Simple Syrup (see page 242)

Put all of the ingredients plus $\frac{1}{2}$ cup ice cubes into a blender. Blend until smooth. Pour into a glass and serve.

Weekend Warrior

An all-natural alternative to protein shakes, the Weekend Warrior, part of our brunch menu, provides steady energy. It is the perfect fuel for home renovation projects, Ultimate Frisbee, or other day-off exertions. MS

1	banana
1	tablespoon almond butter
1	tablespoon flax meal
$\frac{1}{2}$	cup Greek-style vanilla yogurt
2	teaspoons Simple Syrup (see page 242)
$\frac{1}{2}$	cup unsweetened apple juice

Put all of the ingredients plus $\frac{1}{2}$ cup ice cubes into a blender. Blend until smooth. Pour into a glass and serve.

Granola with Nuts, Cardamom, and Orange

MAKES ABOUT 7 CUPS

Making granola at home is easy and provides a chance to bypass the too-sweet commercial varieties. This recipe is flavored with cardamom and coriander, but I've even used yellow curry powder, which imparts an extraordinary color, and cayenne for an unforgettable snap. Raw green pistachios and cashews are less traditional than almonds or walnuts, but they provide a unique appearance and a bolder flavor. MS

¼ cup expeller-pressed canola oil

¼ cup Simple Syrup (see page 242)

½ cup maple syrup

½ teaspoon salt

½ teaspoon ground cardamom

2 teaspoons ground coriander

3 cups old-fashioned rolled oats

1 cup pistachios

1 cup cashews

½ cup brown flax seeds

1 teaspoon freshly grated orange zest

1 cup unsweetened dried cranberries

1. Preheat the oven to 300°F. Line a baking sheet with a silicone baking mat or parchment paper.

2. In a large bowl, mix together the oil, Simple Syrup, maple syrup, salt, cardamom, and coriander. Mix well. Add the oats, pistachios, cashews, and flax seeds. Using your hands, mix well.

3. Put the granola mix in a thin layer on the prepared pan. Bake the granola for 25 minutes. Remove the pan, stir the granola and return to the oven for 15 minutes, until toasted. Remove the granola from the oven and let cool. Add the zest and cranberries. Store in an airtight container at room temperature.

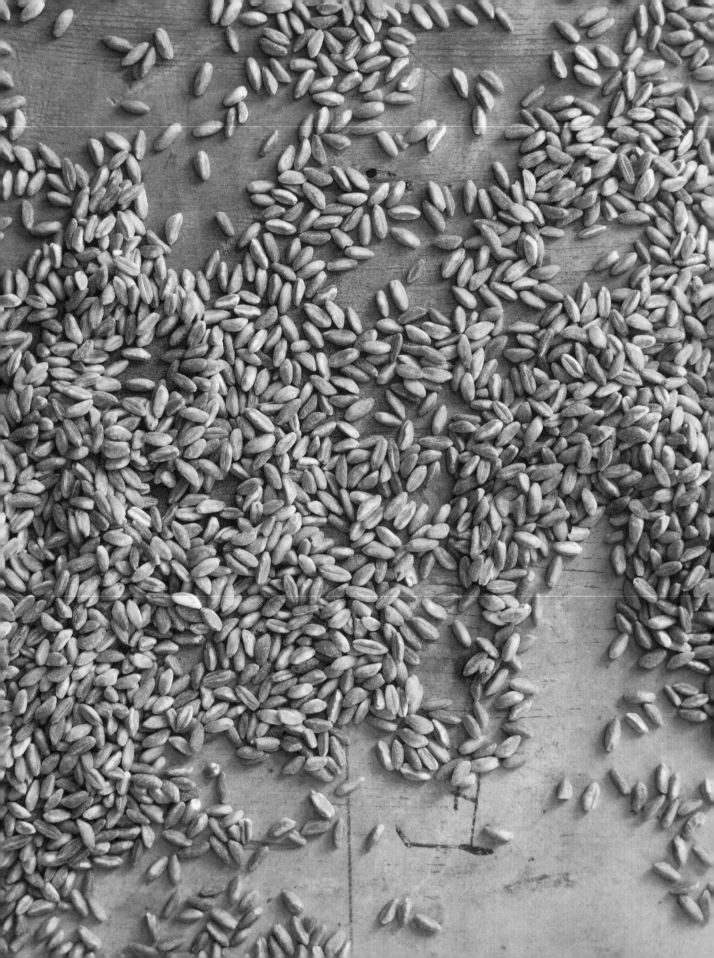

True Whole Grains

You will notice that whole grains are near the base of the Anti-Inflammatory Food Pyramid, but *whole grain* is perhaps the most misused term in discussions of nutrition and in the labeling of manufactured food. Ask the average person to name a whole-grain food, and you'll likely get the response "whole wheat bread."

This conforms nicely with FDA regulations, which allow flour-based products to be labeled "whole grain," but it's nonsense. What's whole about a pulverized grain?

That's why I've tried to popularize the term *true whole grain* to refer to foods that are just that—made of grains that are whole and intact or, at most, broken into a few large pieces—*not* ground into flour. Examples of true whole grains are brown rice, wild rice, corn, barley, wheat berries, and bulgur wheat; buckwheat groats (kasha) and quinoa are grain-like seeds that I use and like.

It's vital to eat grains in their intact form because as such they have a low glycemic index (GI)—a measure of how quickly the body converts them to sugar (glucose). The reason: It takes a long time for digestive enzymes to diffuse through the outer layers of a whole or cracked grain and digest the compacted starch inside. When grains are ground into flour—whether or not some of the bran and germ are included—that starch becomes a fine powder that offers no resistance to enzymatic conversion to glucose. That's why the GI of most whole wheat bread is not much different from that of white bread. Both can cause blood sugar to spike. In many people, frequent blood sugar spikes provoke insulin resistance, weight gain, and increased inflammation throughout the body. That's also why I oppose labeling products made with whole wheat flour "whole-grain foods."

If you find this confusing, here's a simple tabletop test to get a sense of the GI of bread: If you can crush a slice of bread or the inside of a roll into a marble-size lump, that bread will digest quickly and raise blood sugar quickly.

We don't serve that kind of bread (or any bread routinely) at True Food Kitchen, but the restaurant is not a flour-free zone. We serve thin-crust pizzas and make sandwiches with bread that includes cracked grains and seeds, and we provide whole wheat pita bread with our Hummus with Greek Salad (page 44) and Smoked Salmon with Caper Yogurt and Tomato-Onion Relish (page 58). Pita is not very crushable and has a relatively low GI. We use small amounts of flour in some desserts. But we also make liberal use of true whole grains: brown rice, quinoa, and farro, a traditional Italian variety of wheat.

As a lover of pasta, I was pleased to learn that it is a special type of carbohydrate food with a lower GI than bread, especially if it is cooked al dente—resistant to the tooth and therefore also to digestive enzymes. Moderate portions of pasta not drowned in cream and butter are just fine. At True Food Kitchen, we use Asian rice noodles and several other kinds of noodles that are new to many of our customers, such as buckwheat soba and gluten-free spaghetti, which is quite good. AW

Breakfast Tabbouleh

MAKES 4 SERVINGS

When I'm traveling and know that I may not be eating for a while, I start my day with this hearty and filling grain and fruit breakfast. The mint and lime, unusual breakfast flavors, make it particularly refreshing in summer. MS

STRAWBERRY-KIWI PUREE

- 1 kiwi, peeled and cut up
- 6 strawberries, cut up
- 1 teaspoon freshly squeezed lime juice

OAT-WHEAT TABBOULEH

- ½ cup bulgur wheat
- 1 cup old-fashioned rolled oats
- ½ cup diced strawberries
- 1 kiwi, peeled and diced
- ¼ cup chopped pecans or almonds
- ½ cup chopped fresh Italian parsley
- 2 teaspoons chopped fresh mint
- ¼ teaspoon salt
- ⅛ teaspoon freshly ground black pepper

1. Combine all of the Strawberry-Kiwi Puree ingredients in a food processor or blender. Puree until smooth. Strain the fruit mixture through a fine-mesh strainer. Set the strained puree aside.

2. Bring 2 quarts salted water to a boil. Add the bulgur and simmer, stirring occasionally, for 45 to 60 minutes, until tender. Drain well and spread the bulgur in a shallow dish to cool.

3. Preheat the oven to 350°F. Spread the oats on a baking sheet. Toast in the oven for 20 minutes, stirring occasionally, until the oats are lightly browned. Remove and let cool.

4. In a large bowl, combine all of the ingredients and the Strawberry-Kiwi Puree. Divide among serving bowls.

Scrambled Tofu Wraps

Scrambling tofu instead of eggs is a good way to get the health benefits of soy. Turmeric imparts color, and adding black pepper ensures bioavailability of the powerful anti-inflammatory properties of this spice. Vegetables, spices, and soy chorizo make this a hearty breakfast dish, especially when it is wrapped in a whole wheat tortilla. If you like, add $\frac{1}{2}$ cup rinsed and drained canned Anasazi or pinto beans to the scramble. AW

2   **pounds extra-firm tofu, crumbled**

¼   **cup nutritional yeast flakes**

1   **teaspoon salt**

1   **teaspoon ground cumin**

1   **teaspoon ground turmeric**

½   **teaspoon freshly ground black pepper**

1   **tablespoon expeller-pressed canola oil**

1   **small onion, diced**

½   **red bell pepper, diced**

1   **tablespoon extra-virgin olive oil**

1   **(12-ounce) package soy chorizo, crumbled**

1   **medium tomato, diced**

4   **whole wheat tortillas**

8   **avocado slices**

2   **scallions, thinly sliced**

8 to 12 **sprigs cilantro**

1. In a bowl, mix together the tofu, yeast flakes, salt, cumin, turmeric, and black pepper.

2. In a skillet, heat the canola oil over medium-high heat. Add the onion and red pepper, and sauté until the onion is translucent. Let cool, and then add to the tofu mixture. Mix until well combined. (The tofu mixture may be prepared the night before serving.)

3. In a sauté pan, heat the olive oil. Combine the tofu mixture and chorizo in the pan and mix well. Cook over high heat until the mixture turns golden brown and the edges are crispy. Fold in the tomato. Divide the scrambled tofu among the tortillas and top with the avocado slices, scallions, and cilantro sprigs. Roll the tortillas tightly into burritos and cut in half on the bias before serving.

Crustless Quiche with Smoked Sable and Caraway Tofu

MAKES 4 TO 6 SERVINGS

I love quiche, but it's traditionally made with a buttery crust and a filling of eggs, cheese, and cream. This version is made without a crust, uses much less cheese, and substitutes Caraway Tofu in place of cream for richness. Serve right out of the oven or at room temperature, accompanied by a green salad. If you can't find smoked sable, substitute smoked salmon. Use the leftover Caraway Tofu as a spread on crackers or toast. AW

CARAWAY TOFU

Makes 1½ cups

1   (16½-ounce) package silken firm tofu, cut up

2   teaspoons caraway seeds

2   teaspoons freshly grated lemon zest

⅓   cup freshly squeezed lemon juice

¼   cup freshly squeezed orange juice

1   teaspoon salt

1   teaspoon freshly ground black pepper

1. Put all of the Caraway Tofu ingredients in a food processor or blender. Process until smooth and set aside. Store any that you don't use in the refrigerator for up to 3 days.

QUICHE

8   large eggs

½   cup milk

3   slices rye bread, cut into ½-inch cubes

1   tablespoon extra-virgin olive oil

1   leek, chopped

6   ounces asparagus, cut into 1-inch lengths

1   teaspoon salt

4   ounces grated Gruyère or Emmental cheese

1   cup shredded napa cabbage

6 to 8 ounces smoked sable, sliced

2. Preheat the oven to 375°F.

3. In a bowl, whisk the eggs until smooth. Add the milk and whisk thoroughly. Add the bread cubes and let soak for 2 to 3 minutes.

4. In a large ovenproof nonstick skillet, heat the olive oil over medium-high heat. Add the leek and sauté until the pieces begin to soften. Add the asparagus and sauté for 1 minute. Season with the salt.

5. Add the egg mixture to the leeks and asparagus in the skillet. Reduce the heat to medium and stir in the cheese and cabbage. Bake, uncovered, for 25 minutes or until set. Let rest for 5 minutes on a cooling rack.

6. Slide the quiche onto a cutting board and cut into 4 or 6 pieces. Garnish each piece with 2 slices of fish and top with 2 tablespoons of Caraway Tofu.

Carrot-Parsnip-Zucchini Bread

MAKES 2 LOAVES

The idea of melding the sweetness of carrot bread with the moist richness of zucchini bread came about when we were developing the brunch menu in 2009. I was inspired to add parsnip because it contributes a spicy note, somewhere between cinnamon and clove. Apple or pumpkin butter adds moisture. This is a hearty bread, rich with traditional fall spices, that works perfectly on the first chilly days of autumn. MS

1½ cups all-purpose flour

½ cup whole wheat flour

½ cup evaporated cane sugar

1½ teaspoons baking soda

1 teaspoon baking powder

½ teaspoon salt

1 teaspoon ground cinnamon

½ teaspoon ground nutmeg

½ teaspoon ground cloves

1 medium carrot, shredded

1 medium parsnip, shredded

1 small zucchini, shredded

3 large eggs

¾ cup apple butter or pumpkin butter

3 tablespoons extra-virgin olive oil

1 tablespoon vanilla extract

2 tablespoons pumpkin seeds

1. Preheat the oven to 375°F. Oil two 8½ by 4½ by 2½-inch loaf pans with olive oil.

2. In a large bowl, combine the flours, sugar, baking soda, baking powder, salt, cinnamon, nutmeg, cloves, and shredded carrots, parsnip, and zucchini. Mix well. In another bowl, whisk together the eggs, fruit butter, olive oil, and vanilla. Add the wet ingredients to the dry and mix until combined, but don't overmix.

3. Divide the batter between the prepared pans and sprinkle the tops with the pumpkin seeds. Bake for 35 minutes or until a skewer inserted into the center of the bread comes out clean. Let cool on wire racks.

Quinoa Johnnycakes

MAKES 10 TO 12 PANCAKES

New England johnnycakes are usually made with corn flour, but our version uses quinoa instead. The greatest compliment any chef can receive is when a guest says a dish is "the best thing I've ever eaten!" I've heard these very words many times from folks who have just polished off our Quinoa Johnnycakes. We serve them with blueberries in season and bananas the rest of the year. MS

2	cups red quinoa
2	cups all-purpose flour
¼	cup evaporated cane sugar
2	tablespoons plus 1½ teaspoons baking powder
	Pinch of salt
1	teaspoon ground cinnamon
2	cups whole milk
4	large eggs
1	teaspoon vanilla extract
½	teaspoon expeller-pressed canola oil
1	cup blueberries
1	cup Greek-style plain or vanilla nonfat yogurt
	Maple syrup, for serving

1. Bring a saucepan with 4 cups water and 1 teaspoon salt to a boil. Add the quinoa and stir. Lower the heat to a simmer, cover, and cook until the quinoa is dry and fluffy, about 20 minutes. Let cool.

2. Combine the flour, sugar, baking powder, salt, and cinnamon in a large bowl. Whisk well to combine. In another large bowl, combine the milk, eggs, vanilla, and canola oil and whisk to combine. Add the dry ingredients to the wet and blend until just combined. Fold in the cooked quinoa, taking care not to overmix. Let the batter rest for at least 1 hour.

3. Lightly brush the cooking surface of a nonstick pan or griddle with canola oil. Ladle about ⅓ cup of the batter onto the hot pan. Drop 8 to 10 blueberries on top of each pancake. When bubbles form in the batter, flip and cook on the other side until lightly browned. Continue with the remaining batter and blueberries. Serve topped with a dollop of yogurt and maple syrup on the side.

Avoiding Sugar, Fat, and Salt Crutches

People like to think that chefs are superhuman, that it's their extraordinary, rarefied technique that makes some restaurant meals taste so much better than home cooking. Actually, based on what I've seen—and, I must admit, done—during my career, a professional's "amazing skill" is often just excessive use of four ingredients: heavy cream, butter, sugar, and salt.

I've seen chefs in some restaurants add butter to pasta with tomato sauce. I've seen them use mashed potatoes as a binder for cream and butter—adding only enough potatoes to keep the whole thing from turning into a puddle. I've seen polenta made with a half pound of butter per cup of cornmeal; traditionally, polenta has no butter at all. As for sugar, many restaurant bakers add obscene amounts to bread; I've tasted hamburger buns that are about as sweet as a cinnamon roll. Sugar is folded into virtually all restaurant sauces, and it's doubled up in desserts. Salt is overused across the board—in salads, meats, vegetables, everything.

I never went to such extremes, but I'll concede that this attitude influenced me, especially early in my career. So my central aim when I became head chef at True Food was to kick out these crutches. There are obvious health benefits to doing so, but my experience using local, organic ingredients in my own restaurant in San Diego had convinced me that there could be flavor advantages as well. I knew that food could actually taste better if we left these coarse, overbearing flavors behind and pursued a more nuanced, balanced approach.

The human palate can discern five basic tastes: sweet, sour, salty, bitter, and umami, which describes the savory taste of fish, mushrooms, aged cheeses, and soy sauce. Much American cooking is based on only two of these—it is little more than sweetness and saltiness in a fatty "carrier." Our evolutionary past primes us to crave the calorie-dense foods that bear these flavors, so such dishes will always find an audience.

But the good news is that many people today want something deeper, more complex, and real. The modern foodie revolution is a cultural reflection of maturing American taste buds, a recognition that one-note dishes are the culinary equivalent of nursery rhymes.

Masterful cooking combines all five basic flavors artfully and makes controlled use of the fatty taste-transport mechanism. The first step is to use top-quality ingredients, which nearly always taste better than commodity foods. Fresh, organic vegetables are loaded with micronutrients and protective phytonutrients that offer deep, complex flavors. Top-quality organic olive oil contains a significant concentration of polyphenols, which are beneficial to health and provide a peppery bite to many otherwise bland or flat dishes. That bite is entirely absent from lower-quality oils.

Quality, freshness, and naturally balanced flavors are just as vital with animal protein, especially seafood, and sourcing the best is an obsession for me. Mussels in marinara sounds like a gourmet dish, but I assure you, the standard industry motivation for offering this as one of "tonight's specials" is that the mussels are going bad, and drowning

them in salty tomato sauce makes them palatable. Fresh, top-quality fish features a subtle sweetness that requires only a feather-light miso or soy glaze for equilibrium, so that's all we typically use at True Food Kitchen.

Traditional cuisines offer many ways to ramp up the sour, bitter, or umami profiles of dishes. Andy introduced me to the Asian citrus fruit yuzu, which is highly aromatic, tart, and somewhat bitter. It's the foundation of Japanese ponzu sauce, which we use on Snapper Sashimi (page 55); it also goes well with steamed vegetables. I've also become a fan of turmeric, a bright orange relative of ginger with a distinctive earthy taste that offsets, for example, the sweet red peppers in our Scrambled Tofu Wraps (page 23). Sambal oelek, a chile-based condiment popular in Indonesia, Malaysia, and the Philippines, adds some modest heat to our Thai Broth for Hemp-Crusted Trout (page 130) without overpowering the many other flavors of this dish.

As for salt, I've found that the best strategy is not to counter its taste (although sourness can do that to some extent) but simply to reduce its quantity. Restaurants and processed foods have ratcheted up the American craving for salinity; I am committed to reversing that trend. My general rule is to use 50 percent less salt than is traditional in restaurant versions of any given dish. There really isn't magic in any of this, but rather a great deal of experimentation, reading, consulting, tasting, and tweaking. Much of it is attitude—you have to be continually ready to discard an ingredient, or practice, that's been central to your craft for decades when something better comes along. Fortunately, I'm not only ready to do that, but I'm also eager. MS

Carrot-Banana Muffins

MAKES 12 LARGE MUFFINS

My wife, Ally, is always baking something at home, so our kitchen is essentially the True Food pastry R&D (research and development) headquarters. Although she is a professionally trained chef, she has become interested in a new way of cooking and eating that Andy has told us about. The "paleo" or "primal" approach to eating aims to replicate the diet of our hunter-gatherer ancestors: lots of vegetables and moderate amounts of meat, fish, and eggs, along with fruit and small portions of nuts, but little or no grains or dairy. These muffins, which are low in carbohydrates compared to standard versions, fill the bill. MS

2 cups almond flour (also called *almond meal*)

2 teaspoons baking soda

½ teaspoon salt

1 tablespoon ground cinnamon

½ cup unsweetened shredded coconut

3 large eggs

3 bananas, mashed

½ cup (8 tablespoons) unsalted butter, cubed and softened

2 tablespoons raw honey

1 teaspoon apple cider vinegar

1¼ cups pitted and chopped dates

2 medium carrots, shredded

¾ cup chopped walnuts

1. Preheat the oven to 325°F. Lightly oil a 12-cup muffin pan with expeller-pressed canola oil or line with paper liners.

2. In a large bowl, mix together the almond flour, baking soda, salt, cinnamon, and coconut. In another bowl, whisk the eggs, bananas, butter, honey, and vinegar. Stir the wet ingredients into the dry ones. Fold in the dates, carrots, and walnuts. Divide the batter among the muffin cups.

3. Bake for 40 minutes, until golden brown or a skewer inserted into the center of a muffin comes out clean. (Since there's no actual flour, the muffins will not rise significantly.) Cool in the pan on a wire rack for 5 minutes, then turn out the muffins onto the rack and let cool to warm or room temperature.

Antioxidant Berry-Walnut Muffins with Sea Buckthorn Juice Glaze

MAKES 12 LARGE MUFFINS

The term antioxidant *isn't common on restaurant menus, but it appears several times on ours, and our guests have responded positively. These muffins, liberally studded with dried berries and light on sugar, are on our weekend brunch menus. Add them to yours as well. They're made with spelt, an ancient strain of wheat that's richer in nutrients than flours made from modern wheat. A little sea buckthorn juice (see page 223) gives the icing a distinctive tang.* MS

BERRY-WALNUT MUFFINS

1¼ cups spelt flour

1⅓ cups ground dark flax meal

⅔ cup evaporated cane sugar

1 tablespoon baking powder

2 teaspoons ground cinnamon

1½ teaspoons ground nutmeg

3 large eggs

1¾ cups plain soy milk

1 cup fresh or frozen blueberries

¾ cup unsweetened dried cranberries

1 cup coarsely chopped walnuts

SEA BUCKTHORN JUICE GLAZE

1 tablespoon sea buckthorn juice

½ cup confectioners' sugar

½ of an egg white

1. Preheat the oven to 325°F. Lightly oil a 12-cup muffin pan or two 6-cup mini Bundt pans with expeller-pressed canola oil or line with paper liners.

2. In a large bowl, whisk together the spelt flour, flax meal, sugar, baking powder, cinnamon, and nutmeg.

3. In a separate bowl, whisk the eggs. Whisk in the soy milk. Add the wet ingredients to the dry ingredients, mixing until just combined. Fold in the blueberries, cranberries, and walnuts. Let the batter rest for 30 minutes.

4. Fill each muffin cup three-quarters full. Bake for 15 to 20 minutes or until a toothpick comes out clean when inserted in the center of a muffin.

5. While the muffins bake, make the glaze. In a small bowl, whisk together all of the Glaze ingredients.

6. Cool the muffins in the pan for 10 minutes on a wire rack. Turn the muffins out of the pan to cool completely, then drizzle on the glaze.

APPETIZERS

I'm often tempted to make a meal of appetizers
in order to taste more of a restaurant's offerings
without getting too much to eat. Sometimes the
starters appear more interesting and varied than
the main courses. I have no problem putting a meal
together from the recipes that follow. They
include both cold and hot dishes and range from
simple to complex. A selection of colorful, intriguing
appetizers on the table delights the senses and
advertises the inventiveness of kitchens and
cooks. AW

Fava Bean Bruschetta

For Andy's sixty-ninth birthday, I surprised him and his friends with a special family-style Mediterranean feast at his home, and this bruschetta with fava beans was one of the antipasti I served. Bruschetta, a Tuscan appetizer of grilled country bread drizzled with olive oil and rubbed with garlic, comes from the Italian word bruscare, *which means "to char." Fresh fava beans, a sign that spring has arrived, are often paired with Pecorino Toscano, a firm Tuscan sheep's milk cheese.* MS

1 to 1 1/2 pounds fava beans, shelled (about 2 cups after shelling)

5 ounces Pecorino Toscano cheese, cubed

2 tablespoons plus 1/4 cup extra-virgin olive oil

1 1/2 teaspoons freshly grated lemon zest

1 1/2 teaspoons freshly squeezed lemon juice

2 tablespoons chopped fresh mint

2 tablespoons chopped fresh basil

1/2 teaspoon red pepper flakes

1/2 teaspoon salt

12 slices Italian bread

3 garlic cloves, halved

1. Preheat the grill to medium-high or preheat the oven to broil.

2. In a saucepan, bring 4 cups water and 1 teaspoon salt to a boil. Add the shelled beans and cook for 2 minutes. Drain the beans and run under cold water. When cool enough to handle, use your fingers to pop the beans from their husks.

3. When all the beans are shelled, coarsely chop them and put them in a bowl. Toss the beans with the cheese, 2 tablespoons of the oil, the lemon zest and juice, mint, basil, red pepper flakes, and salt.

4. Grill or broil the bread slices until toasted. Brush each slice with some of the remaining olive oil. Then rub each slice with the cut side of a halved garlic clove. Top each bread slice with a spoonful of the bean mixture and serve.

Raw Vegetable Bouquet

The success of this dish hinges almost entirely on the quality and freshness of the produce. A huge bowl of vegetables is pure, elemental food, and it's a fabulous palate cleanser for those weary of culinary conjuring. Just wash the vegetables thoroughly, arrange them like flowers in a vase (with an eye toward harmony in color and shape) and serve very cold with the two dipping sauces. This is a perfect summer appetizer. In winter, use cauliflower of various colors, lightly steamed broccoli or broccolini spears, carrots, and radishes. AW

TZATZIKI DIP
Makes 2¼ cups

- 1 **cup mayonnaise or Vegenaise**
- 1 **cup organic Greek-style plain yogurt**
- 1 **tablespoon plus 1½ teaspoons chopped fresh dill**
- 1 **scallion, white part only, minced**
- 1 **jalapeño chile, seeded and minced**
- 2 **tablespoons plus 1½ teaspoons freshly squeezed lemon juice**
- ½ **teaspoon salt**
- ¼ **teaspoon freshly ground black pepper**

1. In a bowl, whisk together the mayonnaise and yogurt. Whisk in the dill, scallion, jalapeño, lemon juice, salt, and pepper. Cover and refrigerate until ready to use.

VEGETABLE BOUQUET

A wide variety of local, organic, seasonal vegetables, such as cherry tomatoes, lemon cucumbers, sweet baby bell peppers, Persian cucumbers, young carrots, radishes, young celery sticks, jicama spears, and/or romaine hearts (figure at least 1 piece of each of these per person, for 9 or 10 pieces total per person)

Vegetarian Caesar Dressing (page 233)

2. Arrange all of the vegetables in a large chilled bowl or on a cold platter. Serve with the two dipping sauces on the side.

Grilled Halloumi Wraps

MAKES 4 SERVINGS

These wraps remind me of the Italian "grinders" (hero sandwiches) that I used to eat in Boston. I often have one of these wraps for breakfast, but you can cut them into smaller sections and serve them with drinks. Halloumi, a brine-cured cheese that originated in Cyprus, is enjoyed throughout Greece and the Middle East. You can buy cow's milk versions, traditional sheep or goat versions, or halloumi made with milk combinations. All are excellent grilled or sautéed until golden, then topped with onions, tomatoes, lettuce, and pickled hot peppers. Halloumi has a high melting point, so it won't melt easily when grilled or sautéed. Michael gives a method here of preparing your own pickled peppers, but I often use ones from the supermarket. Read the labels to make sure those you buy don't have added color. AW

PICKLED PEPPERS
Makes 1 cup

- 1 cup red wine vinegar
- 1 tablespoon plus 1½ teaspoons evaporated cane sugar
- 1 teaspoon salt
- 16 sprigs thyme
- 2 sprigs oregano
- 1 teaspoon fennel seeds
- 4 to 6 ounces mixed hot peppers, seeded and sliced

HALLOUMI WRAPS

- 12 ounces halloumi cheese, sliced crosswise into 8 pieces
- 4 sprouted grain tortillas
- 1 small red onion, sliced
- 4 to 8 romaine lettuce leaves
- 1 large tomato, sliced
- 2 tablespoons extra-virgin olive oil
- Freshly ground black pepper

1. In a small saucepan, combine the vinegar, sugar, salt, thyme, oregano, and fennel seeds. Place over medium-high heat and cook until the sugar and salt are dissolved. Reduce the heat to low and cook for 20 minutes.

2. Place the peppers in a bowl and pour the pickling liquid through a strainer over the peppers. Place the peppers in the refrigerator to cool. When cooled, transfer the peppers and the liquid to a storage container.

3. Preheat a grill pan over high heat (there is no need to oil it).

4. Grill the cheese on each side until it begins to brown, about 3 minutes. Transfer the cheese to a plate.

5. Arrange the tortillas on a work surface. Place two pieces of the grilled halloumi on each tortilla.

6. Top with the Pickled Peppers (as much or as little as you like), onion, lettuce, and tomato and a light drizzle of olive oil. Sprinkle with black pepper. Roll up tightly, tucking in the ends. Slice each tortilla in half and serve.

Cranberry-Chile Salsa

MAKES 2½ CUPS

Combine roasted chiles with cranberries in this zippy, Mexican-inspired relish, which can replace the usual condiment at your holiday meal. For an appetizer, spread some on pieces of crispbread or serve with carrot and celery sticks. AW

1	**red bell pepper**
2	**poblano chiles**
⅓	**cup evaporated cane sugar**
¼	**cup freshly squeezed orange juice**
2	**cups fresh or thawed frozen cranberries, coarsely chopped**
⅓	**cup toasted and chopped hazelnuts (see page 243)**
2	**tablespoons freshly grated orange zest**
⅓	**cup chopped fresh cilantro**

1. Roast the red bell pepper and poblano chiles by placing them over a gas flame or under a preheated broiler until blackened on all sides. Transfer to a bowl and cover with plastic wrap. Let sit until cool enough to handle. Using your hands, peel off the skins and remove the seeds. It's okay if a bit of the blackened skin remains. Chop the peppers into small pieces.

2. In a saucepan over medium heat, combine the sugar and juice, stirring until the sugar dissolves. Add the cranberries and cook for 1 to 2 minutes. Transfer to a bowl and let cool to room temperature.

3. Combine the roasted red peppers, poblano chiles, hazelnuts, and orange zest with the cranberry mixture. Cover and refrigerate for up to 2 days. Stir in the cilantro just before serving.

Strawberry-Chile Salsa

MAKES 2 CUPS

I have a large strawberry patch at my summer place in British Columbia. I often find myself inundated with berries in June and challenged to find ways to use them. This is one of the best: a medium-hot, bright red salsa flecked with the green of cilantro and chile. Use more or fewer chiles depending on your taste. This is good on its own with chips or raw vegetables, and you can also serve it with grilled fish or chicken. If fresh raspberries are available, try using them in place of strawberries. AW

1	**pint strawberries, diced**
¼	**cup minced onion**
1	**serrano chile, finely chopped, with seeds**
1	**tablespoon freshly squeezed lime juice**
1	**tablespoon chopped fresh cilantro**
	Salt

Combine all of the ingredients and let stand for 15 minutes to blend the flavors before serving.

Cranberry-Chile Salsa

Strawberry-Chile Salsa

Hummus with Greek Salad

MAKES 4 TO 6 SERVINGS

At True Food Kitchen we top our hummus with some traditional Greek salad vegetables. Along with the usual components—chickpeas, tahini, olive oil, lemon juice, garlic, and salt—my version of hummus features Mexican accents, including cumin, jalapeños, and cilantro. The salad dressing adds a European touch via Greek yogurt and French mustard; this dish is a multicultural flavor rush! MS

HUMMUS
Makes 4 cups

- 2 (15 $\frac{1}{2}$-ounce) cans garbanzo beans, rinsed and drained
- 1 large garlic clove, mashed
- 1 small jalapeño chile, seeded and coarsely chopped
- 2 tablespoons plus 1$\frac{1}{2}$ teaspoons tahini
- $\frac{1}{4}$ cup freshly squeezed lemon juice
- Juice of 1 lime
- 1 teaspoon agave nectar
- $\frac{1}{4}$ cup coarsely chopped fresh cilantro
- 1$\frac{1}{2}$ teaspoons ground cumin
- Pinch of cayenne pepper
- $\frac{1}{2}$ teaspoon salt
- $\frac{1}{3}$ cup extra-virgin olive oil

Place the beans, garlic, jalapeño chile, tahini, lemon juice, lime juice, agave nectar, cilantro, cumin, cayenne, and salt in a food processor and blend until it is a smooth paste. Add the olive oil slowly in a thin stream and blend until smooth and well combined. Transfer to a bowl. Store in the refrigerator for up to 3 days.

YOGURT DRESSING
Makes 3 cups

- $\frac{1}{4}$ cup freshly squeezed lemon juice
- $\frac{1}{4}$ cup white balsamic vinegar
- 1 shallot, minced
- 2 tablespoons whole-grain Dijon mustard
- 2 tablespoons agave nectar
- 2 tablespoons chopped fresh oregano
- $\frac{1}{4}$ teaspoon salt
- Pinch of freshly ground black pepper
- $\frac{1}{2}$ cup expeller-pressed canola oil
- $\frac{1}{2}$ cup extra-virgin olive oil
- 1$\frac{1}{2}$ cups Greek-style plain yogurt

Combine the lemon juice, vinegar, shallot, mustard, agave nectar, oregano, salt, and pepper in a blender. Blend for 30 seconds on low speed and then turn the blender to medium speed. Slowly drizzle in the oils and blend until the mixture is emulsified and thick, like mayonnaise. Transfer to a bowl and whisk in the yogurt. Store in the refrigerator for up to 4 days.

GREEK SALAD

- $\frac{1}{4}$ cup thinly sliced cucumber
- $\frac{1}{4}$ cup thinly sliced red onion
- 1 cup cherry tomatoes, halved
- $\frac{1}{4}$ cup Kalamata olives, pitted and quartered
- $\frac{1}{4}$ cup crumbled feta cheese
- 6 tablespoons chopped mixed fresh herbs, such as parsley, oregano, and basil
- 4 pita bread rounds, each cut into 6 wedges, warmed

To serve, put 2 cups Hummus on a plate. Mix the cucumber, red onion, cherry tomatoes, and olives with $\frac{1}{4}$ cup of the Yogurt Dressing. Top the Hummus with this mixture and sprinkle with the crumbled feta and herbs. Serve with the warm pita.

What Is the Anti-Inflammatory Diet?

We all know inflammation when we see it on the body. You can't miss the hot feeling, redness, swelling, and pain at the site of an injury or infection. Inflammation is how the body heals itself, the way it gets more nourishment and immune activity to an area that needs them. But inflammation can also do damage. If it doesn't end when it's supposed to end, if it targets healthy tissues, it causes disease. Persistent, low-level, imperceptible inflammation throughout the body increases risks of heart attack, stroke, Alzheimer's disease, and cancer. Preventing and containing it is the best overall strategy to ensure long-term optimum health and longevity.

Genetics, stress, and exposure to environmental toxins can all influence a person's inflammatory status, but dietary choices are even more important. The reason most people go through life in a pro-inflammatory state is that they are eating pro-inflammatory foods. In general, the industrial and manufactured food that has replaced natural, whole food in the modern diet gives us fats and carbohydrates that increase inflammation while failing to provide nutrients with anti-inflammatory effects.

The natural pigments that color vegetables and fruits; the antioxidants in olive oil, tea, and chocolate; the novel compounds in ginger, turmeric, and other spices and herbs; and the special fats in oily fish all protect our tissues and organs from inappropriate inflammation. Today's mainstream diet is seriously low in these protective elements. At the same time, it is overloaded with fats that promote inflammation: polyunsaturated vegetable oils (especially refined soybean oil, common in industrial food products), margarine and other partially hydrogenated and trans-fats, and fats in the meat of cows and chickens raised on unnatural grain-rich diets. And it gives us carbohydrates mostly in the form of products made from quick-digesting flour and sugar: bread, pastry, cookies, crackers, chips, sugary drinks, and more. These are classified as high-glycemic-load foods, because they raise blood sugar quickly, boost insulin resistance in the many of us who are genetically at risk for it, and increase inflammation, perhaps in several ways. In the past, people ate mostly low-glycemic-load carbohydrate foods, which are digested slowly and do not cause blood sugar to spike, such as whole or cracked (as opposed to pulverized) grains, starchy roots and tubers, beans, and winter squashes.

I have designed an Anti-Inflammatory Diet, using the Mediterranean diet as a template. Much scientific evidence documents the many health benefits of this way of eating, which:

- includes fewer foods of animal origin, except for fish and high-quality dairy products like yogurt and natural cheeses

- relies on olive oil as its main fat

- emphasizes fresh vegetables, fruit, and whole grains

- avoids sugar but allows moderate consumption of alcohol, especially red wine, which has heart-protective effects

I have tweaked the standard Mediterranean diet to increase its anti-inflammatory potential. It is the way I eat and the way I recommend everyone eat for optimum health. I assure you that it is not hard to eat this way and does not mean the end of delicious meals—in fact, you'll enjoy your meals more. The most important rule is simply to avoid refined, processed, and manufactured foods. By taking that one step toward better nutrition, you can significantly reduce the pro-inflammatory pressures of modern living. The True Food Kitchen menu is based on the principles of the Anti-Inflammatory Diet.

Beyond avoiding industrial food, you can keep blood sugar low and stable by choosing slow-digesting forms of carbohydrate. That means eating less bread, white potatoes, crackers, chips, and other snack foods and pastries. It also helps to minimize consumption of tropical fruits such as bananas, pineapple, mango, and papaya. Better choices are whole grains, beans, sweet potatoes, winter squashes, and other vegetables, and cool-climate fruits such as berries, cherries, apples, and pears.

Regarding protein, eat less poultry, which contains pro-inflammatory fats, and more vegetable protein (whole soy foods, beans, lentils, and other legumes) and nuts. Eat fish at least twice a week; choose oily varieties that give you anti-inflammatory omega-3 fatty acids (wild Alaska salmon, sardines, herring, and black cod). We also serve both free-range beef and bison at True Food Kitchen. Because they are grass fed throughout their lives and grass-finished (that is, fattened on grass before slaughter), their fat is higher in omega-3s than that of typical grain-fed factory-farmed animals.

As for what to drink, tea is better than coffee—especially good-quality white, green, or oolong tea. (We do serve organic, fair-trade coffee at True Food Kitchen. If you would like to open a coffee-free restaurant, go ahead, but I suggest self-defense training in anticipation of the inevitable violent customer reaction.) If you drink alcohol, red wine is the best choice.

Because it's tough to pass along all of these ideas in a few sentences, I developed the Anti-Inflammatory Food Pyramid to communicate them in a simple, visual way (see the photograph on page 46 and the "Anti-Inflammatory Diet & Pyramid" at www.drweil.com). It's handed to each diner who enters True Food Kitchen. All of our chefs and servers have committed it to memory. Based on what people tell me in the restaurant and via the web, it's now affixed to thousands of refrigerators around the world.

Many people are thrilled to find that chocolate has a place on the pyramid. It deserves to be there—dark chocolate has greater antioxidant activity than green tea or red wine and can be a valuable addition to any diet. The kind of chocolate I recommend—plain and dark, and at least 70 percent cacao—is relatively low in sugar and provides a healthy fat. Still, it is high in calories and best consumed in moderation, as a treat. That's why chocolate is at the very top of the pyramid, not at the base. AW

Chicken Dumplings with Cilantro-Za'atar Sauce

MAKES 18 TO 20 DUMPLINGS; 4 TO 6 SERVINGS

Za'atar is a Middle Eastern spice mix made of dried herbs ground with sesame seeds, thyme, salt, and dried sumac berries, which have a sour taste. It is used throughout the region to season chicken and lamb or to sprinkle on hummus or olive oil for dipping fresh pita. Recipes vary widely. Lime juice makes this version more of a sauce, a perfect accompaniment to the Asian-style chicken dumpling. MS

CHICKEN DUMPLINGS

- 8 ounces ground chicken
- ½ cup finely chopped bok choy (1 small head)
- 1 scallion, white part only, finely chopped
- 1 tablespoon plus 1½ teaspoons Wok Aromatics (page 237)
- 1 tablespoon low-sodium soy sauce
- 1 teaspoon mirin
- ¼ teaspoon dark sesame oil
- ¼ teaspoon salt
- ⅛ teaspoon freshly ground black pepper
- ¼ cup rice flour
- 1 (12-ounce) package round wonton wrappers

1. Put the chicken, bok choy, scallion, Wok Aromatics, soy sauce, mirin, sesame oil, salt, and pepper in a large bowl. Using your hands, mix well.

2. To make the dumplings, have a small bowl of water with a pastry bush nearby. Lightly dust a baking sheet or platter where you will be placing the filled dumplings with the rice flour. Place 4 wrappers on a clean work surface. Cover unused wrappers with a damp towel or plastic wrap so they will not dry out. Lightly brush the wrappers with water. Place 1 teaspoon of the filling in the center of each wrapper. Moisten the edges with a bit of water and fold over to make a half-moon. Using your fingers, carefully crimp the sealed edges in a scalloped pattern. Repeat with the remaining 3 dumpling wrappers. Continue this process until all the dumplings are made. Place the dumplings on the prepared baking sheet, cover, and refrigerate until ready to cook them.

CILANTRO-ZA'ATAR SAUCE
Makes ⅔ cup

- 1 garlic clove, mashed
- 2 tablespoons Wok Aromatics (page 237)
- 1 tablespoon chopped almonds
- 1 tablespoon toasted sesame seeds
- 1 scallion, green part only, finely chopped
- 1 cup packed fresh cilantro leaves and stems
- 1 tablespoon freshly squeezed lime juice
- 2 tablespoons extra-virgin olive oil
- ¼ teaspoon salt
- ¼ teaspoon freshly ground black pepper
- ½ teaspoon dark sesame oil
- 1 tablespoon unseasoned rice wine vinegar

Continues »

3. Place the garlic, Wok Aromatics, almonds, and sesame seeds in a food processor. Pulse until finely chopped, stopping the machine to scrape down the sides as necessary. Add the scallion, cilantro, and lime juice to the food processor and blend to a puree. Through the feed tube, pour in the olive oil; add the salt, pepper and 2 tablespoons water. Blend until the sauce has the semismooth consistency of pesto. Add the sesame oil and vinegar and blend. Transfer to a bowl and set aside until ready to serve.

TO FINISH

2   **tablespoons expeller-pressed canola oil**

2   **tablespoons toasted sesame seeds**

4. To cook the dumplings, place a steamer in the bottom of a large pot. Add 1 to 1 ½ inches water to the pot. Arrange the dumplings on the steamer, cover, and turn on the heat. Steam for 8 to 10 minutes. Using a slotted spoon and taking care not to burn yourself from the hot steam, transfer the dumplings to a platter flat (bottom) side down.

5. Meanwhile, heat the canola oil in a nonstick skillet over medium-high heat until it shimmers. Using tongs, transfer the steamed dumplings to the skillet, flat side down, and cook until they are golden brown on the bottom. Transfer the dumplings to a paper towel–lined platter and continue until all the dumplings are cooked.

6. Spread the Cilantro-Za'atar Sauce on a platter. Arrange the dumplings on the platter and garnish with the sesame seeds before serving.

Tomato Carpaccio

MAKES 4 TO 6 SERVINGS

Attempting this dish with anything but the freshest possible in-season tomatoes is pointless. Whether you grow your own or buy them at a local farmers' market, using straight-from-the-vine tomatoes is essential. MS

2   pounds tomatoes, sliced
     ¼ inch thick

¼   cup extra-virgin olive oil

2   tablespoons sherry
     vinegar

2   tablespoons finely minced
     shallots

6   fresh basil leaves, sliced

1   tablespoon snipped
     fresh chives

     Salt and freshly ground
     black pepper

Arrange the tomatoes in a decorative pattern on a serving platter. Whisk together the olive oil, vinegar, and shallots in a small bowl. Spoon the dressing over the tomatoes. Sprinkle the basil leaves and chives over the tomatoes. Sprinkle on salt and pepper before serving.

Snapper Sashimi

MAKES 4 SERVINGS

The ever-changing raw fish appetizer is a True Food Kitchen staple, much beloved by regulars. Changing up the fish, sauces, and garnishes helps to keep our menu fresh. The raw fish provides a creative outlet—finding ways to complement such delicate, nuanced flavors is precisely the kind of challenge that inspires talented chefs. Let your fishmonger guide you as to the best sushi-grade raw fish available and use whatever's freshest—ahi, albacore, or butterfish. I like to highlight the buttery strips of fish with seasonal raw, shaved vegetables and a mildly acidic sauce. Nothing says True Food better. MS

PONZU
Makes about ½ cup

2 tablespoons mirin

2 tablespoons Dashi (page 238)

1 tablespoon expeller-pressed canola oil

1 tablespoon yuzu juice

1 teaspoon yuzu kosho

1 teaspoon tamari

1. In a bowl, whisk together all of the Ponzu ingredients. Cover and refrigerate until ready to use.

SASHIMI AND VEGETABLES

1 small fennel bulb, cored and thinly sliced

2 radishes, thinly sliced

2 baby carrots, thinly shaved with a vegetable peeler

2 small or Persian cucumbers, sliced very thinly into rings

12 ounces snapper fillet, thinly sliced

Salt

2 scallions, sliced on the bias

2. Combine the fennel, radishes, carrots, and cucumbers in a bowl and toss well.

3. Divide the fish among cold serving plates. Whisk the Ponzu to blend and spoon 2 to 3 tablespoons sauce over the fish. Divide the vegetables among the plates, sprinkle with salt, and garnish with the sliced scallions before serving.

Tofu-Shiitake Lettuce Cups

MAKES 8 SERVINGS

Lettuce cups filled with chicken and vegetables are served at many Chinese restaurants. Both vegetarians and vegans can enjoy this version made with caramelized tofu and shiitakes and crunchy cashews and jicama. AW

²⁄₃ cup unseasoned rice wine vinegar

½ cup evaporated cane sugar

1 teaspoon salt

16 butter lettuce leaves

1 tablespoon plus 1½ teaspoons expeller-pressed canola oil

5 ounces extra-firm tofu, diced

2 ounces shiitake mushrooms, stemmed and diced

1 tablespoon Wok Aromatics (page 237)

2 cups Teriyaki Sauce (page 235)

1 scallion, chopped

¾ cup diced jicama

¼ cup roasted salted cashews

2¼ teaspoons toasted sesame seeds

1 carrot, shaved into ribbons with a vegetable peeler

1 scallion, thinly sliced

1. In a small saucepan, combine the vinegar, sugar, and salt over medium-high heat and cook until the sugar and salt dissolve. Remove from the heat and set aside.

2. Nestle 1 lettuce leaf partially inside another leaf to make a large cup. Set on a platter and do the same with the remaining lettuce leaves, for a total of 8 cups.

3. In a skillet, heat the oil over medium-high heat until it shimmers. Add the tofu, shiitakes, and Wok Aromatics. Cook until the tofu starts to brown. Lower the heat to medium and add the Teriyaki Sauce. Cook until the sauce is thick enough to coat the back of a spoon, about 5 minutes. Add the chopped scallion, jicama, cashews, and 1½ teaspoons of the sesame seeds and cook for 30 seconds, stirring to combine. Divide the mixture among the lettuce cups.

4. Pour the vinegar mixture into a small bowl, and add the carrot, scallion, and remaining ¾ teaspoon sesame seeds. Toss well and divide among the lettuce cups before serving.

Smoked Salmon with Caper Yogurt and Tomato-Onion Relish

MAKES 4 TO 6 SERVINGS

Greek-style yogurt is smooth and thick, because the liquid whey is strained out. This added density allows you to eat less of it and still be satisfied; it's a great substitute for sour cream or crème fraîche. In this dish, yogurt binds the salmon flakes and other ingredients. Use it as a dip to be scooped with pita chips or as a schmear on a toasted bagel. AW

TOMATO-ONION RELISH

Makes 1 cup

2	medium tomatoes, chopped
1/3	cup Pickled Red Onions (page 241)
2	tablespoons extra-virgin olive oil
1/2	teaspoon chopped fresh Italian parsley
1/4	teaspoon salt

1. In a bowl, gently toss all of the Tomato-Onion Relish ingredients together. Cover and refrigerate until needed.

CAPER YOGURT

2/3	cup Greek-style plain yogurt
2	tablespoons capers, rinsed and chopped
1/4	teaspoon salt

2. In a bowl, whisk together all of the Caper Yogurt ingredients. Cover and refrigerate until needed.

SALMON

6	ounces hot-smoked salmon, cut into 1-inch pieces
	Salt (optional)
24	pita chips, toasted

3. Combine the smoked salmon pieces in a bowl with the Caper Yogurt and 2 tablespoons of the Tomato-Onion Relish. Adjust seasoning with salt if needed. Place the smoked salmon on serving plates and garnish the top with the remaining Tomato-Onion Relish. Serve with toasted pita chips.

Barbecued Shrimp with Mushrooms and Soba Noodles

MAKES 4 SERVINGS

Soba noodles are made from buckwheat and eaten in cold salads, room temperature dishes, and hot soups throughout Japan. They're now found on menus and in markets all over, which is great news because diets rich in buckwheat have been linked to lowered risk of high cholesterol and may help normalize blood pressure. Be sure to make extra, because this dish becomes an excellent cold salad the next day. You may substitute baked tofu for the shrimp. And feel free to use any mushrooms you can find. AW

1 tablespoon expeller-pressed canola oil

3 ounces honshimeji mushrooms, sliced

3 ounces shiitake mushrooms, stemmed and sliced

3 ounces oyster mushrooms, sliced

3 ounces maitake mushrooms, sliced

1 teaspoon grated fresh ginger

5 ounces soba noodles, cooked and drained

½ cup Dashi (page 238)

2 teaspoons freshly squeezed lemon juice

⅓ cup Carrot-Miso Vinaigrette (page 233)

1 cup shredded napa cabbage

16 large shrimp, peeled and deveined

⅓ cup Asian Barbecue Sauce (page 234)

¼ cup sliced-on-the-bias scallions, green part only

1 tablespoon toasted sesame seeds

1. Preheat the grill to high.

2. In a nonstick skillet, heat the oil over medium-high heat until it shimmers. Add all of the mushrooms and cook over high heat until they begin to brown. Add the ginger and soba noodles and toss to combine. Add the Dashi and lemon juice and let reduce until most of the liquid has evaporated, about 3 minutes. Add the Carrot-Miso Vinaigrette and cabbage and toss together. Remove the skillet from the heat and cover. Keep warm until the shrimp are cooked.

3. Brush the shrimp on both sides with Asian Barbecue Sauce and place on the grill. Baste occasionally with the sauce as they cook. Grill for 3 to 5 minutes on each side. (This may also be done in a grill pan on the stovetop.)

4. Divide the warm mushrooms and soba noodle mixture among serving plates. Put 4 shrimp on each plate and garnish with the scallions and sesame seeds before serving.

SALADS

Back in the 1970s, when I told people I was a vegetarian, a response I got more than once was, "I couldn't eat salad three times a day." Of course, my diet was much more varied than that, but the funny thing is: I could eat salad three times a day—if it were varied and made with the freshest ingredients. In parts of Asia, salad is popular at breakfast. In the Middle East, people often begin the day with raw vegetables, yogurt, and olives. Many diners at True Food Kitchen order one of the salads in this chapter as a main course—for brunch, lunch, or dinner. AW

Kale Salad

MAKES 8 SERVINGS

Here's the signature dish of True Food Kitchen. People who never imagined eating raw kale quickly become devoted. Unlike most salads, this one gets even better in the fridge overnight. Make the extra effort to find Tuscan kale—also sometimes labeled as black kale, cavolo nero, or dinosaur kale—as its deeper color and more complex flavor really lift this into the salad stratosphere. AW

½ cup extra-virgin olive oil

¼ cup freshly squeezed lemon juice

3 garlic cloves, mashed

½ teaspoon salt

Pinch of red pepper flakes

2 bunches kale (about 14 ounces), ribs removed and leaves sliced into ¼-inch shreds

½ cup finely grated Grana Padano or Parmigiano-Reggiano cheese (grated on a Microplane)

2 tablespoons toasted whole wheat bread crumbs

Grana Padano or Parmigiano-Reggiano cheese shavings, for garnish

1. In a salad bowl, whisk together the oil, lemon juice, garlic, salt and red pepper flakes. Add the kale and toss well to coat. Let the salad sit at room temperature for 10 to 30 minutes. Add the grated cheese and bread crumbs and toss again.

2. Garnish with the cheese shavings before serving. Cover any leftovers and refrigerate for up to 2 days.

How Americans Are Learning to Love Raw Kale

Who would have thought Americans would go for raw kale?

I hated greens when I was growing up, and kale was definitely not on my "yum" list. I first got into it when I began spending summers in British Columbia, where everyone grows kale and keeps it going into the fall and winter. (Most varieties are very cold tolerant and taste even better after some frost.) I found

that I liked it stir-fried or lightly steamed, seasoned with a little vinegar. But when, on a trip to a remote northern island, I was served a salad that contained raw kale, I picked it out and left it on the edge of my plate. It was too tough and bitter for me.

That was Scotch kale, the common curly blue-green variety that has thick leaves and definitely needs frost to make it taste good. I grew it once in my winter garden in Arizona but then replaced it with the Red Russian variety, the texture of which I prefer. I ate it regularly until warm weather came, mostly stir-fried in olive oil; often flavored with garlic, onions, and hot red pepper flakes; and sometimes as a main dish mixed with pasta, capers, and grated Parmigiano-Reggiano. I also started growing Italian black kale (lacinato kale or cavolo nero), which is more heat tolerant and tasty even without winter cold. I liked the color, shape, and flavor of its leaves. Still, I had no interest in eating any kind of kale raw.

Then, when traveling in Tuscany one fall, I had *the* salad and fell in love. I took careful note of the ingredients and made it for Sam Fox and his wife the first time they came to dinner at my house: sliced raw black kale dressed with extra-virgin olive oil, fresh lemon juice, fresh garlic, salt, black pepper, and red pepper flakes, all tossed with grated Pecorino Toscano cheese and toasted bread crumbs.

The secret of the preparation is to let the kale sit in the dressing for at least 15 minutes before you serve it; the lemon juice and salt make the leaves tender and tasty, eliminating any bitterness. Soon I was growing only black kale and using most of it raw. I made this traditional Italian salad for many guests; everyone loved it.

Still, I wondered how it would do on the True Food Kitchen menu. I grew more optimistic when, shortly before our Phoenix opening, we prepared sample dishes for New York food editors. One, from *Glamour* magazine— who presumably had consumed a great many salads— proclaimed it the best salad she had eaten in her life.

For most Americans, kale has epitomized all that's dreadful about healthy food. Undeniably nutrient-dense— rich in vitamins and minerals and organosulfur compounds that have been linked to lowered cancer risk—it's generally regarded as boring when cooked and virtually inedible when raw. Yet True Food's Kale Salad is the most popular item we serve, one of our signature dishes. Many customers ask for the recipe (see page 64), which we are pleased to give them, and many report back that they make it regularly at home. The only adjustment we made to the traditional preparation is to substitute Grana Padano or Parmigiano-Reggiano cheese for the Pecorino Toscano, which Sam thought would be too "sheepy" and sharp for our clientele.

Bob McClendon, who grows our organic black kale on his farm in Peoria, Arizona, reports that he now grows ten times more than he did before the restaurants in Phoenix and Scottsdale opened. Part of it goes to our kitchens' walk-ins; but even more is snapped up by his farmers' market customers seeking to make "that salad from True Food," some of whom report eating it daily. With the opening of the southern California locations, our demand for organic black kale skyrocketed, stimulating growers to plant much more. I believe that True Food Kitchen is responsible for helping make this vegetable—unknown in this country until very recently—increasingly popular today.

Not long ago, a mother with a son and a daughter about seven and five came up to me in the Phoenix restaurant. "Tell Dr. Weil what your favorite thing to eat here is," she said to the girl, who was too shy to answer. Her brother spoke for her: "Kale salad! Kale salad!" he said with great enthusiasm. That made me very happy.

If folks in Arizona, which is hardly a bastion of veg-heads, can learn to love raw kale, it is only a matter of time before true love for it blooms across the land.

Spring Salad with Aged Provolone

The perfect start to a springtime picnic or barbecue, this salad really hits all corners of your palate. I love how the slight bitterness of the artichokes works with the acidity of the lemon and the sweetness of the basil. Raw artichokes are often paired with Parmigiano-Reggiano, but I like the sharp smokiness of aged provolone. MS

LEMON BASIL DRESSING
Makes 1½ cups

- ¼ cup freshly squeezed lemon juice
- 1 tablespoon white balsamic vinegar
- 2 teaspoons Dijon mustard
- 1 garlic clove, mashed
- ¼ teaspoon salt
- ⅛ teaspoon freshly ground black pepper
- 1¼ cups extra-virgin olive oil
- 1 tablespoon chopped fresh basil leaves

1. Combine the lemon juice, vinegar, mustard, garlic, salt, and pepper in a medium bowl. Whisk together and then slowly drizzle in the oil. Add the basil right before serving. Leftover dressing may be stored in the refrigerator for up to 3 days.

SALAD

- 1 cup Pickled Cucumbers (page 241)
- 1 zucchini or yellow squash, thinly sliced
- 1 small fennel bulb, cored and thinly sliced
- 1 medium artichoke, outer leaves, fuzzy part, and choke removed, thinly sliced
- 1 small head Treviso or other radicchio, torn into pieces
- 2 cups mixed baby greens
- 3 ounces sugar snap peas, slivered
- 2 tablespoons pitted and quartered Picholine or other green olives
- 4 ounces aged provolone cheese, shaved with a vegetable peeler

2. In a salad bowl, combine the Pickled Cucumbers, zucchini, fennel, artichoke, radicchio, greens, sugar snap peas, and olives, and toss well. Add several tablespoons of the Lemon Basil Dressing and toss, adding more dressing as necessary. Divide among salad plates and top with the shaved provolone before serving.

Fattoush

Fattoush is the Arabic term for a salad made with stale bread and vegetables. I love bread salads, but typically they become too much about the bread and dressing. The modest proportion of whole wheat pita adds a little texture to the real stars of this dish, the asparagus, celery root, and tomatoes. The roasted red pepper dressing also makes a great dip for raw or cooked vegetables. MS

ROASTED RED PEPPER AND GARLIC VINAIGRETTE
Makes 1 cup

- 1 **red bell pepper**
- ¾ **cup extra-virgin olive oil**
- 8 **garlic cloves, peeled**
- ¼ **cup balsamic vinegar**
- ¼ **teaspoon red pepper flakes**
- ¼ **teaspoon salt**
- ¼ **teaspoon freshly ground black pepper**

1. Roast the bell pepper under a broiler or over a gas flame until blackened. Place in a bowl and cover with plastic wrap to loosen the skins. Let cool to room temperature, and then peel and seed the pepper.

2. Put ½ cup of the olive oil and the garlic cloves in a small saucepan over medium heat. When it begins to slowly bubble, reduce the heat to the lowest setting and let simmer until the garlic turns light golden brown, about 4 minutes. Remove from the heat and let cool.

3. Place the roasted bell pepper in a blender. Add the cooked garlic cloves, reserving the oil. Add the balsamic vinegar, red pepper flakes, salt, and pepper to the blender. Puree to a smooth paste. Drizzle in the roasted garlic olive oil and the remaining ¼ cup olive oil. Blend until smooth and well incorporated. Adjust seasonings as desired. Leftover dressing may be stored in the refrigerator for up to 5 days.

Continues »

ROASTED ASPARAGUS AND CELERY ROOT

8 ounces asparagus, trimmed and cut into ½-inch pieces

1 medium celery root, trimmed and cubed

1 tablespoon extra-virgin olive oil

Salt and freshly ground black pepper

4. Preheat the oven to 375°F. Line a baking sheet with a silicone baking mat or aluminum foil.

5. Arrange the asparagus and celery root on the prepared sheet and toss with the oil, salt, and pepper. Bake for 15 to 20 minutes, until the asparagus and celery root can be pierced with a fork. Set aside to cool.

SALAD

2 (8-inch) whole wheat pita bread rounds, torn into pieces the size of quarters

1 cup cherry tomatoes, halved

½ cup fresh Italian parsley leaves

¼ cup fresh dill fronds

12 fresh mint leaves

¼ cup pitted and slivered Picholine or other green olives

2 ounces (about 3 cups) spinach leaves

2 ounces (about 3 cups) arugula

Salt and freshly ground black pepper

6. In a large bowl, combine the pita, roasted asparagus and celery root, ½ cup of the Roasted Red Pepper and Garlic Vinaigrette, and the remaining salad ingredients, tossing to mix well. Let sit for 5 minutes so the pita softens a bit. Add more dressing if needed, and serve.

Greek Salad

Make this only with the ripest garden tomatoes. If your cucumbers are young, you can leave the immature seeds in; otherwise scrape out the seed cavities. The vegetables should be in sizable chunks for this salad. Many varieties of feta are available: some sour, some salty, some creamy and mild. Try different kinds to find the one you like most. AW

OIL AND VINEGAR DRESSING
Makes 1¼ cups

1 cup extra-virgin olive oil

¼ cup red wine vinegar

2 large garlic cloves, mashed

2 tablespoons dried oregano

Salt and freshly ground black pepper

1. Combine all of the ingredients in a jar, shake well, and let stand for 30 minutes to let the flavors blend. Leftover dressing may be stored in the refrigerator for up to 5 days.

SALAD

2 teaspoons salt

1 medium red onion, halved and thinly sliced

3 medium tomatoes, cut into wedges

1 cucumber, peeled and cut into chunks

1 green bell pepper, seeded and sliced

1 red bell pepper, seeded and sliced

¼ cup chopped fresh basil

½ cup pitted and halved Kalamata olives

2 tablespoons chopped fresh Italian parsley

6 ounces feta cheese, sliced

6 lemon wedges

2. In a bowl, combine the salt with 2 cups water and add the red onion slices. Let the onions soak for 15 minutes, then rinse and drain well.

3. In a large bowl, toss the tomatoes, cucumbers, and bell peppers with the basil and enough of the Oil and Vinegar Dressing to coat the vegetables well. Adjust the seasonings as desired. Arrange in a high mound on a serving platter; top with the olives, parsley, feta, and lemon wedges; and serve.

Gado-Gado

Gado-gado is an Indonesian salad. Infinite variations dressed with peanut sauce are sold in street vendor stalls, cafés, and the finest restaurants. Serve it cold on a hot summer day as a first course or as a side dish to Southeast Asian–inspired meals. Add other fruits like watermelon or honeydew for a twist. MS

GADO-GADO DRESSING
Makes 1½ cups

- 2 garlic cloves, mashed
- 1 shallot, finely chopped
- 1 Thai red chile, chopped
- 2 tablespoons evaporated cane sugar
- ¼ cup Thai or Vietnamese fish sauce
- ¼ cup freshly squeezed lime juice
- 3 tablespoons unseasoned rice wine vinegar
- ⅓ cup Thai peanut sauce
- 1 medium carrot, shredded

1. Put the garlic, shallot, chile, sugar, fish sauce, lime juice, vinegar, and 3 table-spoons water into a blender or food processor. Blend until smooth. Add the peanut sauce and blend until smooth. Pour into a container, stir in the shredded carrot, cover, and refrigerate until needed. Shake well before using. Leftover dressing may be stored in the refrigerator for up to 3 days.

SALAD

- 2 medium tomatoes, seeded and cut into ½-inch wedges
- 1 small cucumber, thinly sliced on the bias
- 1 small carrot, shaved on a vegetable peeler
- 1 peach, pitted and diced
- 1 small green papaya, peeled, pitted, and sliced into ¼-inch strips
- 1 small mango, peeled, pitted, and diced
- 1 small red bell pepper, seeded and cut into ¼-inch strips
- ¼ cup fresh cilantro leaves
- 1 cup pea sprouts (optional)
- ¼ cup chopped salted peanuts

2. In a large bowl, combine the tomatoes, cucumber, carrot, peach, papaya, mango, and red pepper. Toss with ½ cup of the Gado-Gado Dressing. Taste and add more dressing as necessary. Divide the salad among serving plates. Top with the cilantro leaves, sprouts (if using) and peanuts before serving.

Roasted Butternut Squash, Apple, and Pomegranate Salad

MAKES 4 TO 6 SERVINGS

Although I haven't cooked professionally in years, I invented this salad on opening day at the original True Food Kitchen. With roasted squash, apples, pomegranate seeds, and toasted walnuts, it's become a favorite on our autumn and winter menus. SF

1   butternut squash, peeled, seeded and cut into bite-size pieces

2   tablespoons extra-virgin olive oil

1   teaspoon salt

6   ounces (about 9 cups) mixed baby greens

1   apple, such as Fuji, Gala, or Honeycrisp, cored and sliced

½   cup Balsamic Vinaigrette (page 232)

5   ounces goat cheese, crumbled

¼   cup walnuts, toasted and chopped (see page 243)

¼   cup pomegranate seeds

1. Preheat the oven to 400°F. Line a baking sheet with a silicone baking mat or aluminum foil.

2. In a bowl, toss the squash with the olive oil and salt. Arrange the squash in a single layer on the prepared sheet. Bake for 20 to 25 minutes, until the squash is lightly browned. Remove from the oven and let cool for 10 minutes.

3. In a salad bowl, toss together the mixed greens, squash, apple, and Balsamic Vinaigrette. Top with the goat cheese, walnuts, and pomegranate seeds before serving.

Salad as a Main Course

The easiest way to turn a salad into a main course is to serve more of it and add protein. At lunch, many of our guests ask for a portion of grilled chicken or salmon on top of a salad, which makes for a satisfying, low-carb midday meal—colorful ingredients, contrasting textures, and plenty of protective phytonutrients. Cold cooked shrimp, crab, or lobster also work well, as does baked, pressed tofu for vegetarians and vegans.

Another possibility is to add crumbled, chunked, or shaved cheese. My favorites are blue cheese, mild soft goat cheese, Gruyère, Manchego, and Parmesan. Or add cooked root vegetables like potatoes, carrots, and beets; toasted nuts; edamame or other beans; or whole grains like quinoa or couscous. All make green salads more interesting and more filling.

It is very enjoyable to sit down to a main course of crisp, fresh greens tossed with a light but flavorful dressing and fortified with the right amount of animal or vegetable protein. One can still feel virtuous, even after eating an ample main-course portion of such a salad. AW

Chicken-Farro Salad

Farro is a chewy, nutty strain of Italian wheat that adds whole-grain goodness and an unexpected texture to salad. One summer, we took this dish—with sweet dates, roast chicken, Manchego cheese, Marcona almonds, and farro tossed with a champagne vinaigrette—off the menu. We brought it back two weeks later in response to an onslaught of letters and e-mails from customers. If you have leftover chicken, this is a great way to get another meal out of it. If not, season some boneless chicken breasts with olive oil, salt, and pepper. Bake at 350°F for 25 to 30 minutes. Let the chicken cool before cutting it into pieces. Of course, you can leave the chicken out for a vegetarian option. MS

½ cup farro

6 ounces (about 9 cups) mixed baby greens

1½ cups leftover cooked chicken, cut into strips

⅓ cup unsweetened dried cranberries

⅓ cup chopped dates

2 ounces Manchego cheese, shaved with a vegetable peeler

¼ teaspoon salt

¾ cup Champagne Vinaigrette (page 232)

¼ cup chopped Marcona almonds

1. Bring 2 quarts salted water to a boil. Add the farro and simmer, stirring occasionally, for 45 to 60 minutes, until tender. Drain well and spread the farro on a shallow dish to cool.

2. In a salad bowl, combine the greens, chicken, cooled farro, cranberries, dates, cheese, and salt. Toss with ½ cup Champagne Vinaigrette, adding more as needed. Divide the salad among plates and garnish with the almonds before serving.

Chopped Sashimi Salad

Capturing the flavors of my favorite sushi rolls was the inspiration behind this chopped salad. The combination of cucumber, avocado, sesame seeds, raw saku tuna, and miso along with edamame and baby greens is clean and flavorful. Saku is sushi-grade tuna, typically frozen at sea with powerful blast freezers that minimize cell disruption and lock in the freshness. Thaw it in the refrigerator overnight; don't thaw it under running water or worse, in a micro-wave, as it can get mushy. You can toss all the ingredients together or compose them individually for a striking presentation. MS

12 ounces sushi-grade tuna, diced

⅓ cup Pickled Cucumbers (page 241)

¼ cup shelled frozen edamame, cooked according to package directions

1 teaspoon toasted sesame seeds

½ teaspoon salt

1 avocado, pitted, peeled, and sliced

4 ounces mixed baby greens

⅓ cup Carrot-Miso Vinaigrette (page 233)

Toss the tuna, cucumbers, edamame, sesame seeds, and salt together in a bowl. Arrange the tuna mixture, avocado slices, and greens on plates. Pass the Carrot-Miso Vinaigrette on the side.

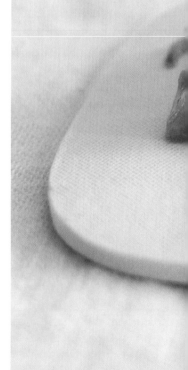

Quinoa Tabbouleh

MAKES 4 TO 6 SERVINGS

Traditional tabbouleh is made with bulgur wheat. Quinoa, a native grain of the high Andes, is higher in protein than bulgur wheat, gluten-free, and easy to cook. The red variety is particularly attractive in this vegetable-and-herb-packed salad. This makes a satisfying main course for lunch. AW

1	pound beets
2	cups red quinoa
½	cup extra-virgin olive oil
¼	cup freshly squeezed lemon juice
3	garlic cloves, mashed
½	teaspoon salt
	Pinch of red pepper flakes
⅓	cup chopped fresh Italian parsley
¼	cup chopped fresh mint
3	scallions, chopped
2	ounces arugula
½	pomegranate, seeds removed and reserved
¼	cup chopped Marcona almonds

1. Preheat the oven to 350°F. Line a baking sheet with aluminum foil. Pierce the beets in a few places with a fork. Bake for 45 minutes to 1 hour, until tender and easily pierced with a knife. Remove the beets from the oven and allow to cool for 20 minutes. Use paper towels to peel off the skins or your hands will be pink for days. Cut into cubes and set aside.

2. Meanwhile, bring 4 cups salted water to a boil. Add the quinoa. Lower the heat, cover, and simmer for 20 minutes, until the quinoa is dry and fluffy. Let cool.

3. In a salad bowl, whisk together the oil, lemon juice, garlic, salt, and red pepper flakes. Add the beets, quinoa, parsley, mint, scallions, and arugula and toss well to combine. Divide the salad among serving plates. Top with pomegranate seeds and almonds before serving.

Moroccan Chicken Salad

MAKES 6 SERVINGS

Roasted chicken, cashews, and a tasty dressing with curry and yogurt make this a North African–inspired salad. (Use leftover chicken or season some boneless chicken breasts with olive oil, salt, and pepper. Bake at 350°F for 25 to 30 minutes. Let the chicken cool before cutting it into pieces.) This salad is good on its own, served with whole-grain crackers, but we also make it into an open-faced sandwich at True Food using our fresh-baked whole-grain bread. MS

1	cup plain yogurt
½	cup mayonnaise
⅓	cup honey
2	teaspoons grainy mustard
1	tablespoon freshly squeezed lime juice
1	teaspoon curry powder
½	teaspoon salt
½	teaspoon freshly grated lime zest
2	tablespoons chopped fresh cilantro
2	cups leftover boiled or roasted chicken, diced
1	small celery stalk, diced
½	cup chopped roasted salted cashews
½	cup golden raisins
¼	cup diced jicama
3 or 4	scallions, white part only, chopped
12	romaine lettuce leaves

1. In a large bowl, combine the yogurt, mayonnaise, honey, mustard, lime juice, curry powder, salt, lime zest, and cilantro. Whisk well to combine. Add the chicken, celery, cashews, raisins, jicama, and scallions and mix thoroughly.

2. Serve over the romaine lettuce leaves. Or chop the lettuce and mix it into the salad.

Tomato and Watermelon Salad

Use a combination of red and yellow watermelon and red, yellow, and orange tomatoes for a stunning presentation. The necessary freshness of the base ingredients can come only from a farmers' market or, better yet, your own backyard garden. MS

1   **pound red watermelon, rind removed and cut into 1½-inch chunks**

1   **pound yellow watermelon, rind removed and cut into 1½-inch chunks**

4   **heirloom tomatoes, halved**

1   **pint cherry tomatoes, halved**

2   **tablespoons extra-virgin olive oil**

2   **tablespoons white balsamic vinegar**

½   **teaspoon salt**

    Pinch of freshly ground black pepper

2   **tablespoons small fresh basil leaves**

4   **ounces mild, soft goat cheese, such as Montrachet, crumbled**

¼   **cup chopped roasted unsalted cashews**

Divide the watermelon pieces and tomatoes among salad plates. Drizzle each plate with the olive oil and vinegar. Season with the salt and pepper. Top with the basil, goat cheese, and cashews before serving.

Scallops with Kale Pesto

MAKES 4 SERVINGS

This salad features a satisfying mix of vegetables and protein. It will fill you up but leave you light on your feet. The emerald green kale pesto provides a striking color contrast. AW

3 tablespoons extra-virgin olive oil

16 sea scallops

Salt and freshly ground black pepper

4 medium tomatoes, cut into bite-size chunks

3 bell peppers (red, yellow, and orange), seeded and thinly sliced

2 cups corn kernels, shaved from 2 ears corn

1 cucumber, peeled, seeded (if seeds are mature), and thinly sliced

1 jalapeño chile, seeded and thinly sliced

1 shallot, thinly sliced

¼ cup extra-virgin olive oil

3 tablespoons champagne vinegar

½ cup Kale Pesto (page 234)

4 ounces mild, soft goat cheese, crumbled

1. Heat the olive oil in a nonstick skillet over medium-high heat until it shimmers. Season the scallops with salt and pepper. Sear the scallops on both sides for 1 to 2 minutes, but don't overcook. Transfer to a platter.

2. In a large bowl, combine the tomatoes, bell peppers, corn, cucumber, jalapeño, and shallot. Drizzle the oil and vinegar over them, season with salt and pepper, and toss. Divide among serving plates. Add the scallops and garnish each scallop with about a teaspoon of the Kale Pesto. Sprinkle on the goat cheese before serving.

SOUPS & CHILIS

Soups can be thin or thick, hot or cold, smooth or chunky. They can be served in small portions at the beginning of a meal or in larger portions as main courses. The recipes in this section illustrate the great variety of soups served at True Food Kitchen as well as several chilis ("soupy entrées"). Feel free to experiment with them. Soups offer the home cook a chance to be creative, use up ingredients on hand, and bring deeply satisfying dishes to the table. AW

Sweet Potato–Poblano Soup

MAKES 12 CUPS; 6 SERVINGS

Soups are ideal for serving nutrient-dense foods. I often just chop a bunch of vegetables up and simmer them in water or stock to make a flavorful vegetable broth. This version involves roasting for deeper flavor, but it is still easy and quick to prepare. Paying close attention to the seasonality of your main ingredients will drastically improve results. MS

1 large sweet potato, peeled and diced

1 small onion, diced

½ cup corn kernels, shaved from 1 ear corn

1 small carrot, diced

1 small fennel bulb, diced

4 garlic cloves, mashed

1 poblano chile, seeded and diced

2 tablespoons extra-virgin olive oil

1 tablespoon chili powder

1 teaspoon ground cumin

1 teaspoon dried oregano

¼ teaspoon cayenne pepper

½ teaspoon ground turmeric

½ teaspoon salt

½ teaspoon freshly ground black pepper

½ cup white wine

1 (14-ounce) can light coconut milk

¼ cup chopped fresh cilantro

2 or 3 scallions, thinly sliced

1. Preheat the oven to broil. Line a baking pan with aluminum foil.

2. Toss the sweet potato, onion, corn, carrot, fennel, garlic, and poblano together in a large bowl. Add the olive oil and toss to coat. Arrange the vegetables in a single layer in the prepared pan and broil for 5 to 7 minutes. Remove the pan and toss the vegetables. Cook for another 5 to 7 minutes, or until browned on top. Take care not to burn the vegetables.

3. Transfer the vegetables to a large pot. Stir in the chili powder, cumin, oregano, cayenne, turmeric, salt, pepper, wine, and 3 quarts water. Bring to a simmer over medium-high heat. Reduce the heat and simmer the soup for 45 minutes.

4. Remove the soup from the heat and whisk in the coconut milk. Ladle the soup into bowls and garnish with the cilantro and scallions before serving.

Tomato-Bread Soup

Pappa al pomodoro from Tuscany is a simple way to use up stale bread. Roasted tomatoes add the necessary depth of flavor. The soup is as filling as a serving of pasta, so portion it accordingly and pair it with a green salad. MS

3   **large tomatoes, halved widthwise and cored**

2   **tablespoons plus ¼ cup extra-virgin olive oil**

½   **teaspoon salt**

    Freshly ground black pepper

2   **garlic cloves, mashed**

1   **small loaf Italian bread, torn into 1-inch pieces (about 6 cups; can be stale)**

½   **teaspoon red pepper flakes**

½   **cup Kale Pesto (page 234)**

3   **cups grated Parmigiano-Reggiano cheese**

1. Preheat the oven to 300°F. Line a baking sheet with aluminum foil.

2. Place the tomatoes, cut side up, on the baking sheet and drizzle with 2 tablespoons of the olive oil. Season with the salt and black pepper. Roast the tomatoes until they are soft, about 2 hours. Let cool.

3. Scoop the tomato pulp and juices from the skins into a bowl. Discard the skins. Using a fork, break the tomato flesh into bite-size pieces. (This may be done a day or two in advance. Store the tomatoes in the refrigerator.)

4. Heat the remaining ¼ cup olive oil in a large pot over medium heat, add the garlic, and sauté for 1 minute. Add the tomatoes and their juices. Bring to a simmer, cover, and cook for 10 minutes.

5. Stir in 5 cups water, the bread, and red pepper flakes. Bring back to a simmer, then remove from the heat. The soup should be thick but not mushy. (Add more water if necessary.) Add the Kale Pesto and adjust the seasoning with salt.

6. Ladle the soup into bowls and top each serving with 3 tablespoons cheese. Place the remaining cheese on the table for those who want to add more.

Butternut Squash–Apple Soup

Slow-roasting the squash, apple, and onion together makes them tender and flavorful. Cashew milk makes the soup rich and creamy. You can vary the recipe by adding different spice combinations, such as curry powder and turmeric, ground cumin and coriander, nutmeg and allspice, or smoked paprika. AW

1 medium butternut squash, peeled, seeded, and cut into 1-inch pieces (about 12 cups)

4 or 5 Granny Smith or other tart apples, peeled, cored, and cut into wedges (about 5 cups)

1 large onion, diced

2 garlic cloves, mashed

2 teaspoons expeller-pressed canola oil

1 teaspoon salt

½ teaspoon cayenne pepper

3 cups Cashew Milk (page 239)

1. Preheat the oven to 400°F. Line a baking sheet with aluminum foil.

2. Put the squash, apples, onions, and garlic in a large bowl and toss with the oil, salt, and cayenne. Arrange the mixture in a single layer on the prepared baking sheet and roast until tender and lightly browned, about 45 minutes.

3. Allow the ingredients to cool for 20 minutes, then transfer to a standing blender (or use an immersion blender). Hold the lid down firmly with a clean, folded towel over it. Start on low speed and blend until smooth. Add up to 1¼ cups room temperature water, ¼ cup at a time, until the soup has the desired consistency. Return to the pot, whisk in the Cashew Milk, reheat if needed, and adjust the seasoning. Ladle into bowls and serve hot.

Immunity Soup

Modern research shows that astragalus root, a Chinese herb long used to ward off colds and flu, has powerful immune-enhancing properties. The sliced, dried root is available online and in herb stores; it is nontoxic and adds a pleasant, sweet taste when simmered in soups. Shiitake mushrooms also boost immunity and have an antiviral effect. Garlic is an antibiotic and ginger a natural anti-inflammatory agent. AW

1½ teaspoons extra-virgin olive oil

2 large onions, thinly sliced

3 garlic cloves, mashed

1 tablespoon minced fresh ginger

4 ounces shiitake mushrooms, stemmed and thinly sliced (about 2 cups)

2 large carrots, thinly sliced on the bias

2½ pieces astragalus root (about 15 inches total)

10 cups Mushroom Stock (page 238)

2 tablespoons tamari or low-sodium soy sauce

Salt (optional)

2 cups broccoli florets

½ cup chopped scallions

1. In a large pot, heat the olive oil over medium heat. Add the onions, garlic, and ginger and sauté until soft and translucent. Add the shiitakes, carrots, astragalus root, and Mushroom Stock. Bring to a low boil. Reduce the heat and simmer for 45 minutes.

2. Add the tamari and adjust the seasoning with salt if needed. Add the broccoli florets and cook until tender, about 2 minutes.

3. Remove the astragalus root pieces. Ladle the soup into bowls and garnish with the scallions before serving.

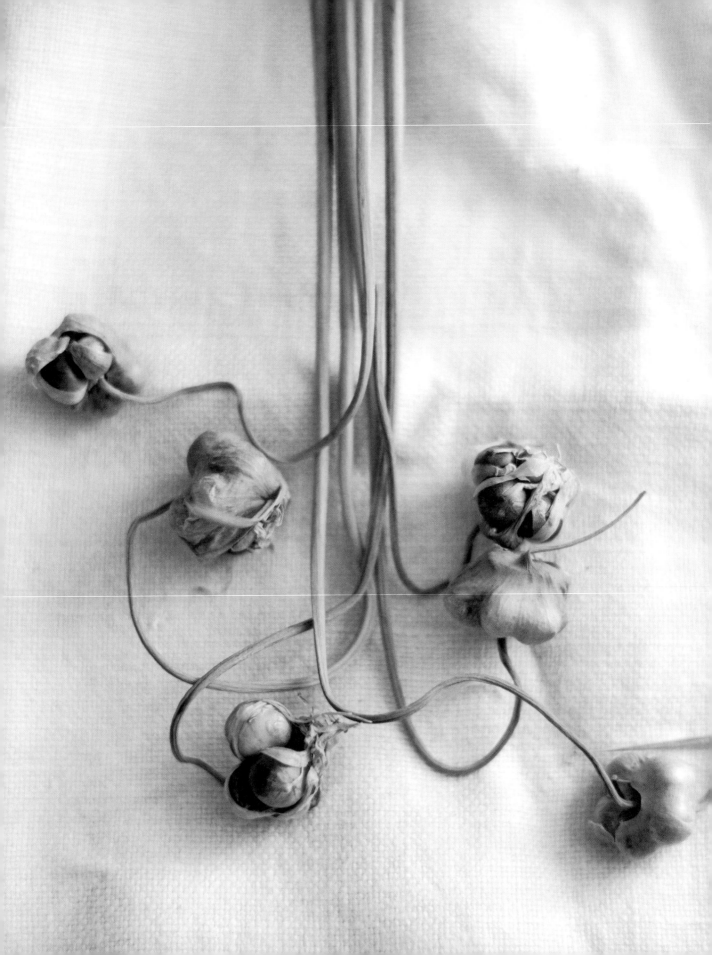

The Way of the Garlic Press

Andy uses garlic often in his home kitchen, always fresh, much of it from his garden. Typically, he uses a garlic press to mash the cloves into dishes he prepares. He's a great fan of good Swiss-made versions and would not be without one.

Chefs like me, on the other hand, always mince garlic, often showing off our knife skills as we do so. When Andy and I started cooking together and inventing dishes for the True Food Kitchen menu, I let him know I had no use for such a gadget.

Andy told me he prefers mashed, rather than minced, garlic for two reasons. First, he said, the flavor is more pronounced. Second, he believes the health benefits of mashed garlic are greater. This is because the compound responsible for garlic's odor, flavor, and medicinal properties—allicin—isn't present in fresh garlic until it is cut and exposed to air. The greater the surface area of the cut garlic, the greater the production of allicin, and mashed garlic has a much greater surface area than does minced.

Andy further argued that often, when he ordered Kale Salad (page 64) at the restaurant, he couldn't taste enough garlic in the dressing, certainly not as he tasted it when he made the salad at home. I told him that the cooks were following the recipe exactly and that the garlic was fresh and of good quality. I made new batches of dressing for him to try, but he still felt the flavor of garlic was lacking. After much experimentation, we agreed that the difference had to do with his use of a garlic press.

I began using one and had to admit that it did improve the taste of my food. I also appreciated the greater health-protective effects of more allicin. Fresh garlic is a powerful antibiotic that also protects heart health, may reduce cancer risk, and helps control inflammation.

Some time later, when Andy and I did a cooking demonstration in Newport Beach, I told him my wife had given me a large-capacity garlic press for my birthday and that I'd been using and enjoying it, both at home and in the restaurant. I am now, officially, a rebel; I've never met another professional chef willing to use one. To my fellow professionals, I would only say, give it a shot: Your career will survive, and your food will taste better. MS

Curried Cauliflower Soup

This rich soup is healthy, vegan, and quick to prepare. It's good hot or cold and keeps well if you don't plan to serve it all at once. I use orange cauliflower rather than white when I can find it, for its higher content of beta-carotene. Cashew milk makes the soup deliciously creamy. This is a good way to get the anti-inflammatory benefit of turmeric. Garnish each bowl with caramelized onions and bright green cilantro for a beautiful presentation. AW

1/3 cup raw cashews

2 teaspoons extra-virgin olive oil

1 medium onion, diced

1 large head cauliflower, cut into 1-inch pieces

1 (14-ounce) can light coconut milk

2 tablespoons curry powder

1 teaspoon ground turmeric

1 teaspoon ground cumin

1 teaspoon evaporated cane sugar

1/4 teaspoon ground cinnamon

Salt

Caramelized Onions (page 240), for serving

1/4 cup chopped fresh cilantro

1. Put the cashews in a blender and blend until finely ground. Add 3/4 cup water and blend for 2 minutes. Pour the cashew mixture through a fine-mesh strainer into a bowl, pressing on the solids with the back of a spoon. Discard the solids.

2. In a large pot, heat the olive oil over low heat. Add the onion and sauté until golden. Add the cauliflower, coconut milk, strained cashew milk, curry powder, turmeric, cumin, sugar, cinnamon, and salt as needed. Add enough water to cover. Bring to a low boil, reduce the heat, and simmer until the cauliflower is tender, about 10 minutes.

3. Blend the soup with an immersion blender until the desired consistency is reached. If using a standing blender, allow the mixture to cool for 20 minutes. Pour the soup into the blender. Hold the lid down firmly with a clean, folded towel over it. Start on low speed and blend until the soup is smooth. Return to the pot and reheat if serving hot. Ladle into bowls and garnish with the Caramelized Onions and cilantro before serving.

Heirloom Tomato Gazpacho

This True Food Kitchen version of the Spanish classic is one of our most popular dishes during the broiling summer months in Phoenix. Nothing tastes better on a sizzling day than ice-cold fresh vegetables in a chilled bowl. Paradoxically, adding a little hot spice to food helps your body cool itself as well. This dish is a good base for experimenting with different chiles, as their flavors emerge cleanly. MS

4 to 5 pounds chopped heirloom tomatoes	
1	**(20-ounce) can diced tomatoes**
2	**celery stalks, diced**
1	**poblano chile, stemmed, seeded, and chopped**
1	**red bell pepper, diced**
1	**small red onion, diced**
½	**cup diced jicama**
1	**medium cucumber, peeled, seeded, and diced**
¼	**cup chopped fresh Italian parsley**
1	**tablespoon chopped fresh cilantro**
⅓	**cup red wine vinegar**
2	**tablespoons extra-virgin olive oil**
2	**teaspoons vegetarian Worcestershire sauce**
1½	**teaspoons green Tabasco sauce**
2	**teaspoons salt**
2	**teaspoons ground coriander**
1	**teaspoon ground cumin**
½	**teaspoon cayenne pepper**

Combine all of the ingredients plus ¼ cup cold water in a large bowl and mix well to combine. Transfer 3 cups of the mixture to a blender. Blend until smooth, and then return to the bowl. Mix well, cover, and refrigerate. Serve cold.

Chicken Sausage
and Roast Fennel Soup

MAKES 12 CUPS; 6 SERVINGS

A hearty soup like this one is appreciated in sunny Arizona, but it would seem absolutely lifesaving in the depths of a New England winter. It is loaded with flavorful vegetables and homemade chicken sausage. I make a large batch, have a meal, let the remainder cool thoroughly, and then portion it into pressure-sealable plastic bags. I stack these in the freezer for an impromptu supper or hot lunch. Making your own chicken sausage is the best option (an easy method is included here), but you can use top-quality chicken sausages offered at gourmet supermarkets and natural foods stores. For a vegan version, substitute 6 ounces chopped Tofurky Italian sausage for the chicken sausage. MS

1   pound ground chicken

1   medium onion, diced

2   garlic cloves, mashed, plus 1 garlic clove, mashed (keep them separate)

2½ teaspoons salt

1½ teaspoons red pepper flakes

1   tablespoon fennel seeds

½   teaspoon cayenne pepper

2½ teaspoons caraway seeds

½   teaspoon ground cumin

¼   teaspoon fresh thyme leaves

½   teaspoon fresh oregano leaves

1   small carrot, diced

1   medium fennel bulb, diced

1   small parsnip, diced

2   small boiling potatoes, such as red bliss, diced

¾   teaspoon smoked paprika

3   tablespoons extra-virgin olive oil

1   (14-ounce) can San Marzano tomatoes, chopped, with juice

½   cup chopped fresh Italian parsley

1. Place the ground chicken in a stainless steel bowl. Add 1 tablespoon of the diced onion, 2 of the garlic cloves, 1 teaspoon of the salt, 1 teaspoon of the red pepper flakes, 1 teaspoon of the fennel seeds, cayenne, ½ teaspoon of the caraway seeds, cumin, thyme, and oregano. Using your hands, mix so all the ingredients are well distributed throughout. Wash your hands. Cover and refrigerate the sausage mixture until needed.

2. Preheat the oven to 400°F. Line a baking sheet with aluminum foil.

3. In a large bowl, combine the remaining onion, carrot, fennel bulb, parsnip, and potatoes. In a spice grinder, combine the remaining 1 clove garlic, ½ teaspoon red pepper flakes, 2 teaspoons fennel seeds, and 2 teaspoons caraway seeds. Pulse to combine the spices and grind the seeds into smaller pieces. If you don't have a spice grinder, use the flat side of a chef's knife to smash the spices. Add the ground spices, smoked paprika, remaining 1½ teaspoons salt, and 1 tablespoon of the olive oil to the vegetables and toss to coat evenly. Arrange the vegetables in a single layer on the prepared baking sheet. Roast the vegetables in the oven until lightly browned, about 25 minutes, tossing them once while cooking. Remove from the oven.

4. In a large pot, heat the remaining 2 tablespoons olive oil over medium-high heat. Add the chicken sausage and brown, using a wooden spoon to break up the sausage into pieces the size of grapes. Add the roasted vegetables, tomatoes, and 8 cups water. Bring the soup to a low boil, reduce the heat to a simmer, and cook for 30 minutes. Stir in the chopped parsley and serve hot.

Southwestern Bison Meatball Soup

MAKES ABOUT 12 CUPS; 6 SERVINGS

Meatballs are the quintessential comfort food at my house. I spice them up with Southwestern flavorings and serve them Italian-style, garnished with Parmigiano-Reggiano shavings and chopped parsley. Using ground bison and turkey instead of beef or pork lowers the fat content and amps up the flavor. Grass-fed bison is widely available at supermarkets and natural foods stores. The soup and the meatballs can be served together as in this recipe, but each can also stand on its own. Try the meatballs over pasta or piled on whole wheat rolls for hero sandwiches. MS

SOUP

2	tablespoons Annatto Oil (page 239)
1	carrot, chopped
1	large onion, chopped
1	small zucchini, cubed
1	cup cubed jicama
3	tablespoons tomato paste
9	cups Chicken Stock (page 237)
¾	cup quinoa
1	(28-ounce) can pureed San Marzano tomatoes
1	tablespoon chili powder
2	teaspoons ground cumin
2	teaspoons dried oregano
1	teaspoon salt
¼	teaspoon freshly grated orange zest

1. In a large pot, heat the Annatto Oil over medium heat. Add the carrot and sauté for 2 minutes. Add the onion and sauté for another 2 minutes. Add the zucchini and jicama and sauté for 2 minutes. Add the tomato paste and sauté for 2 minutes. Add the stock, quinoa, tomato puree, chili powder, cumin, oregano, and salt. Bring to a simmer and cook for 20 minutes.

2. Stir in the orange zest. Taste and adjust salt and pepper as needed. Simmer for an additional 5 minutes. Set aside and keep warm or cool quickly and store in the refrigerator.

Continues»

BISON MEATBALLS

Makes 20 small meatballs

- 8 ounces ground bison
- 4 ounces ground turkey
- 3 tablespoons extra-virgin olive oil
- 1 small onion, minced
- 3 garlic cloves, mashed
- 2 teaspoons tomato paste
- 1 teaspoon salt
- 1/4 teaspoon plus a pinch of freshly ground black pepper
- 1/8 teaspoon red pepper flakes
- 1/2 teaspoon ground cumin
- 1/2 teaspoon dried whole oregano leaves
- 1/2 teaspoon chili powder
- 1/4 teaspoon freshly grated orange zest
- 2 dashes of Tabasco or other hot sauce
- 3 large eggs
- 1/4 cup whole wheat bread crumbs
- 1 teaspoon chopped fresh oregano
- Manchego cheese, shaved with a vegetable peeler
- 1/4 cup chopped fresh cilantro

3. Preheat the oven to 400°F. Line a baking sheet with a silicone baking mat or aluminum foil.

4. Combine the bison and turkey in a stainless steel bowl. Heat 1 tablespoon of the olive oil in a skillet over medium heat. Add the onion and garlic and sauté for 1 minute. Stir in the tomato paste, 1/2 teaspoon of the salt, and a pinch of black pepper and cook for 2 minutes. Remove the pan from the heat and let cool. When cool, add the vegetables to the ground meat. Using your hands, mix in the red pepper flakes, cumin, dried oregano, chili powder, orange zest, Tabasco, eggs, bread crumbs, fresh oregano, remaining 1/2 teaspoon salt, and remaining 1/4 teaspoon black pepper. Mix well so all the ingredients are evenly distributed.

5. Using your hands, shape the meat into golf ball–size meatballs. Heat the remaining 2 tablespoons oil in a skillet over medium-high heat. When the oil is hot, add the meatballs and cook to brown on all sides. Once browned, place the meatballs on the prepared baking sheet. Bake until cooked, about 20 minutes.

6. To serve, ladle the soup into bowls and add 5 to 7 meatballs to each bowl. Top with shaved Manchego and cilantro before serving.

Bison Chili

Bison is an excellent source of quality protein, relatively low in saturated fat and best when grass fed and grass finished, which gives the meat a favorable ratio of omega-3 to -6 important fatty acids. The subtle spiciness and depth provided by cinnamon and cocoa give this dish a full, rounded flavor. Making this chili a day in advance allows the flavors to come together harmoniously. Serve with grilled whole wheat tortillas, Manchego shavings, a dollop of Greek yogurt, and a sprinkling of cilantro. MS

3	tablespoons extra-virgin olive oil
12	ounces ground bison
½	teaspoon salt
½	teaspoon freshly ground black pepper
1	small onion, finely chopped
2	garlic cloves, mashed
1	tablespoon ground cumin
1	tablespoon chili powder
1	tablespoon pure ancho chile powder
½	teaspoon red pepper flakes
1	cup canned diced San Marzano tomatoes
1	(15-ounce) can white beans, rinsed and drained
½	cup Chicken Stock (page 237)
1	(1-inch square) piece 70% dark chocolate
1	teaspoon dried oregano
½	teaspoon paprika
⅛	teaspoon ground cinnamon
1	teaspoon salt
½	teaspoon chopped fresh oregano

1. In a large pot, heat the olive oil over medium-high heat. Add the ground bison and season with the salt and pepper. Cook, stirring occasionally, to brown the meat, 3 to 5 minutes. Add the onion and sauté for 2 minutes. Add the garlic and continue cooking for another 2 minutes while stirring. Add the cumin, chili powder, ancho chile powder, and red pepper flakes. Stir and cook for another minute. Add the tomatoes, beans, and Chicken Stock. Stir well and bring to a simmer. Reduce the heat to low and simmer for 30 minutes, stirring often to prevent sticking.

2. Add the chocolate, dried oregano, paprika, cinnamon, and salt. Stir and let simmer for another 15 minutes. Add the fresh oregano. Adjust the seasoning. Simmer for 5 minutes.

3. Ladle into bowls and serve with desired accompaniments. If not serving immediately, let the chili cool, and then refrigerate for up to 4 days or freeze for up to 1 month.

V Woman, GF Man, Seek Restaurant...

One of the most remarkable changes in American food culture in the past fifty years has been the mainstreaming of once-fringe food philosophies. When I was a kid in the 1950s, vegetarians (including my aunt Rebecca) were kooks. In restaurants, there was no tofu, tempeh, quinoa, shiitake mushrooms, or even yogurt. Eating out was safe and predictable. Meat was the usual main course.

In the intervening years, three intersecting trends—emerging affluence, a growing emphasis on individuality, and an explosion in nutrition science—fostered explosive growth of these diets:

- vegetarian: abstaining from animal-flesh foods

- vegan: abstaining from all animal-derived foods, including dairy, eggs, and even honey

- gluten-free: abstaining from foods containing gluten, a protein found in wheat, barley, and rye that is sometimes also used to stabilize or thicken processed foods

- low-fat: minimizing foods high in dietary fat such as whole dairy, marbled meat, and bacon

- low-carb: minimizing foods high in carbohydrates, such as bread, potatoes, and pasta; a more recent variant, known as *paleo* or *primal*, focuses on minimizing categories of foods, especially grains, that were not part of the human diet before the invention of agriculture

Which—if any—of these is the "right" diet is a complex question. A lifetime of research has persuaded me that my Anti-Inflammatory Diet (see page 47) is the best choice for most people. It is largely vegetarian but emphasizes fish, too, and allows some other animal protein, while remaining low in unhealthy fats and carbs. It is also easy to follow for those who restrict their gluten intake, as gluten-rich grains are only a small and easily avoided component.

So while our entire True Food Kitchen menu falls under the rubric of my Anti-Inflammatory Food Pyramid, it also contains many individual dishes that fit each of these specialized diets. One of the best decisions we made in assembling the menu is using abbreviations (with a key at the bottom of the page) to help diners identify which offerings fit their food philosophy: "v" for vegan, "veg" for vegetarian, and "gf" for gluten-free. (Low-fat and low-carb are not "absolute" restrictions, so we don't label our dishes as such.) This has worked out well, because these days virtually any group of four or more people includes one member on a restricted diet.

As for diet trends, Michael says he's getting more and more low-carb/paleo requests, which he finds really easy to accommodate. "We can add a turkey burger patty to any salad. One of my personal favorite things to eat is the Kale Salad with added grilled chicken or salmon and some avocado for extra, healthy fat. It easily becomes a meal."

In other words, the '50s are over. We no longer have to conform. Human beings are not all the same, and it's appropriate that we should be able to tailor our restaurant experience to fit our unique physiologies, ethics, or tastes. At True Food, we work hard to make that easy. AW

Azuki, Tempeh, and Corn Chili

MAKES 12 CUPS; 6 SERVINGS

Japanese azuki beans are high in protein and easy to digest, and they cook faster than almost any other dried bean. They make an outstanding addition to chili. This is a Mexican-inspired version, loaded with vegetables and posole, which is the white hulled corn (hominy) that is ground for tortillas and tamales. Smoked tempeh adds even more protein and flavor. I like to make a large quantity of this chili; it keeps well and improves with reheating. You can serve it with such accompaniments as chopped onions, lettuce, tomato, hot sauce, and, if you like, your favorite shredded or crumbled cheese. AW

¼ cup extra-virgin olive oil

1 (12-ounce) package smoked tempeh, cut into 1-inch pieces

1 small onion, diced

2 garlic cloves, mashed

6 to 8 tomatillos, peeled and chopped

2 or 3 medium tomatoes, peeled, seeded, and diced

1 medium zucchini, diced

1 cup corn kernels, shaved from 1 ear corn

1 medium yellow summer squash, diced

2 Anaheim chiles, roasted, peeled, and diced

2 poblano chiles, diced

¾ teaspoon minced jalapeño chile

¾ teaspoon minced Fresno chile

½ cup canned azuki beans, rinsed and drained

1 cup canned white posole, rinsed and drained

1 tablespoon ground cumin

2 teaspoons dried oregano

⅛ teaspoon chili powder

1¾ teaspoons salt

1 teaspoon freshly grated orange zest

1 cup fresh cilantro leaves, chopped

1. Heat a stockpot over medium-high heat and add the olive oil. Add the tempeh and sauté until lightly browned. Add the onion and sauté until it begins to soften. Add the garlic and sauté for 1 minute. Add the tomatillos, tomatoes, zucchini, corn, squash, all the chiles, beans, posole, cumin, oregano, chili powder, salt, and orange zest, and mix well. Simmer for 20 minutes.

2. Turn the heat to the lowest setting and let simmer for another 20 minutes. Serve in bowls garnished with the cilantro.

Spicy Shrimp and Asian Noodles

MAKES 4 SERVINGS

Many Americans know ramen only as the eight-for-a-dollar packets of noodles and seasoning favored by impoverished students. When we called this dish "Shrimp Ramen" on our menu, we wanted to evoke Japan's rich gourmet ramen tradition, but our guests didn't see it that way. Once we changed the name to "Spicy Shrimp and Asian Noodles," it immediately began selling. Like crazy. MS

RAMEN BROTH
Makes 10 cups

- **10 cups Chicken Stock (page 237) or Mushroom Stock (page 238)**
- **3 or 4 dried shiitake mushroom caps**
- **3 sprigs cilantro**
- **2 tablespoons chopped fresh ginger**
- **2 tablespoons pounded and chopped lemongrass**
- **¼ cup low-sodium soy sauce**
- **1 teaspoon honey**
- **¾ teaspoon salt**
- **¼ teaspoon crushed spicy dried chile, such as arbol**

1. Combine all of the Ramen Broth ingredients in a large pot and bring to a simmer over medium heat. Reduce the heat and cook for 1 hour.

2. Remove the broth from the heat and let cool for 30 minutes.

3. Strain the broth through a fine-mesh sieve and return to the pot; discard the solids. Keep the broth at a simmer while preparing the noodles and eggs. Leftover broth may be refrigerated for up to 4 days or stored in the freezer for up to 1 month.

PICKLED JALAPEÑOS
Makes ½ cup

- **⅔ cup unseasoned rice wine vinegar**
- **½ cup evaporated cane sugar**
- **1 tablespoon salt**
- **2 or 3 jalapeño chiles, sliced**

4. In a small saucepan, combine the vinegar, sugar, and salt. Place over medium-high heat and simmer until the sugar and salt dissolve. Pour the mixture over the sliced jalapeños in a bowl. Cover and refrigerate until ready to use.

Continues»

NOODLES, SHRIMP, AND VEGETABLES

1 pound soba noodles, cooked in boiling water for 2 minutes, then drained

1 tablespoon distilled white vinegar

4 large eggs

12 large shrimp

3 ounces honshimeji mushrooms, stemmed

2 ounces snow peas, sliced on the bias

1 cup sliced spinach leaves

½ cup Pickled Red Onions (page 241)

5. Divide the cooked noodles among serving bowls.

6. Add the white vinegar to a saucepan of water and bring to a boil. Break the eggs one at a time into the water. Poach the eggs to desired doneness, 4 to 5 minutes. Using a slotted spoon, remove the eggs and put one in each bowl.

7. While the eggs are cooking, bring the Ramen Broth to a simmer, add the shrimp and mushrooms to it, and cook at a simmer for 4 to 6 minutes. Using a slotted spoon, remove the shrimp and mushrooms from the broth and place on top of the noodles. Add the snow peas to the broth and cook for 1 minute. Using a slotted spoon, remove the snow peas and arrange on the soba noodles. Repeat with the spinach leaves. Gently ladle the broth into the bowls. Garnish with the pickled onions and jalapeños.

Seafood Fideo

Fideo means "noodle" in Spanish and also refers to a Mexican soup made with toasted pasta cooked in the broth. This version combines spaghetti (gluten-free or not) and a selection of seafood. I make the broth a day in advance to allow the flavors to marry. Buy only the freshest seafood from a good source. If you are not able to get the varieties we suggest or if you don't care for clams or mussels, omit them and substitute your own fresh favorites. MS

2	medium tomatoes, chopped
1	small onion, chopped
1	large jalapeño chile, seeded and chopped
2	garlic cloves, mashed
5	tablespoons Annatto Oil (page 239)
8	ounces spaghetti, broken into 2-inch pieces
1	(8-ounce) bottle clam juice
1/8	teaspoon saffron
1/2	teaspoon smoked paprika
4	ounces black cod, cut into 8 pieces
8	large shrimp, shelled and deveined
16	littleneck or other small clams, scrubbed
1/2	fennel bulb, thinly sliced
1/2	cup fresh or frozen peas
4	ounces fresh cooked crabmeat
2	cups thinly sliced kale strips

1. Place the tomatoes, onion, jalapeño, and garlic in a blender and puree until smooth.

2. In a skillet, heat 3 tablespoons of the Annatto Oil over medium heat. Add the pureed vegetables and cook for 5 minutes.

3. In a large pot over medium heat, heat the remaining 2 tablespoons Annatto Oil. Add the spaghetti and sauté until golden. Add the clam juice, 6 cups water, saffron, and smoked paprika. Stir in the pureed vegetables. Cook until the spaghetti is al dente. Using a slotted spoon, transfer as much spaghetti as possible from the pot to warm bowls. Cover and keep warm. Add the black cod, shrimp, clams, fennel, and peas to the pot. Cover and cook over medium heat for 3 minutes. Add the crab and kale and heat through. Discard any clams that don't open. Divide the seafood and broth over the pasta in the bowls and serve hot.

SEAFOOD, POULTRY & MEAT

The True Food Kitchen menu offers a number of animal protein options: fish, shellfish, chicken, turkey, bison, and dairy products. We are careful in our selection of these foods, paying attention to concerns about both health and sustainability. In many dishes, like the curry and rice bowls, animal protein is one of many ingredients and can be omitted or replaced with tofu. When it is the featured ingredient, it is always paired with expertly cooked vegetables. AW

Salmon *Kasu*

Kasu, the lees (residue) from brewing vats of Japanese rice wine (sake), comes packaged in soft, beige cakes, available at Japanese and some Asian groceries and online sites. It has a tantalizing, yeasty aroma and adds a deep, intriguing flavor to marinades and pickles. To avoid overcooking salmon or any fish, take it off the heat before you think it's done. AW

¼   cup sake

⅓   cup *kasu* (sake lees)

¼   cup white (*shiro*) miso

1   tablespoon dark brown sugar

1   tablespoon low-sodium soy sauce

4   (6-ounce) salmon fillets

1   teaspoon expeller-pressed canola oil

1. Heat the sake in a saucepan over low heat for 5 minutes. Remove from the heat and put the sake, *kasu*, miso, ¼ cup water, sugar, and soy sauce in a food processor. Blend until the mixture has the consistency of wet sand.

2. Spread one-third of the paste over the bottom of a baking pan large enough to hold the salmon in a single layer. Arrange the salmon on top of the paste and spread the rest on top of the salmon. Cover and refrigerate for 12 to 48 hours.

3. Preheat the oven to broil or preheat the grill to medium-high. Scrape the kasu paste from the salmon and pat the fish dry with paper towels. Lightly brush the fish with the oil and broil or grill the fish until just done, 10 to 12 minutes. Serve immediately.

Albacore Tuna with Sweet and Sour Sauce

Albacore, or white tuna, is emerging as a popular alternative to other varieties of tuna that are quickly becoming unsustainable. Because of its smaller size and quick maturity, albacore caught via "pole and troll" in the north Pacific Ocean is certified sustainable by the Marine Stewardship Council. It is also known to have lower mercury levels than comparable tuna species. Albacore has a tendency to dry out if overcooked, so watch it carefully. Grapeseed oil is recommended because it has a high smoking point and a neutral taste. Keep a bottle in the refrigerator for searing fish and poultry. Chinese black vinegar, sometimes labeled as Chinkiang vinegar, is an essential ingredient in this dish. Steamed rice and sautéed greens go well with as accompaniments. MS

SWEET AND SOUR SAUCE
Makes ³/₄ cup

- ⅓ cup low-sodium soy sauce
- 3 tablespoons plus 1½ teaspoons Chinese black vinegar
- ¼ cup evaporated cane sugar
- 4 garlic cloves, mashed

1. Whisk together all of the Sweet and Sour Sauce ingredients in a bowl.

TUNA

- 4 (5- to 6-ounce) pieces albacore tuna loin
- 2 teaspoons salt
- 2 teaspoons freshly ground black pepper
- 3 to 6 tablespoons grapeseed oil

2. Remove the tuna loin from the refrigerator 30 to 45 minutes before cooking and let it come to room temperature. Using your hands, press the salt and pepper into the fish on all sides. Wash your hands.

3. In a large nonstick pan, heat 3 tablespoons of the oil over high heat until it shimmers. Place the tuna in the hot oil, 2 pieces at a time. Sear on each side to desired doneness, but don't overcook. Tuna is best when rare in the middle. Transfer the cooked tuna to a serving platter. Cook the remaining 2 pieces, adding more oil to the pan if necessary.

4. Slice the tuna into 1-inch pieces. Serve accompanied by the Sweet and Sour Sauce.

Eat Your Fish

In 1970, at age 28, I became a lacto-vegetarian. That meant giving up most foods of animal origin except dairy products.

The change of diet agreed with me. I lost weight, enjoyed better health, and was able to eat varied, pleasurable meals. But by the mid-1980s, I needed a change. My way of eating made it difficult to eat out and to travel (especially to Japan, one of my favorite places). Because I could not ignore mounting scientific evidence in favor of the health benefits of eating fish, I slowly added it to my diet. I found that I appreciated fish all the more for having avoided it for so long. I've never regretted the change.

Populations that eat fish regularly live longer and have less chronic disease than populations that don't. This is probably because fish—especially fatty varieties from cold northern waters—are the best source of omega-3 fatty acids, the healthy fats our bodies need every day for optimum physical and mental health. Lack of sufficient omega-3 fatty acids constitutes a serious and widespread nutritional deficiency in our population, one that contributes to excessive inflammation throughout the body and raises risks of many diseases.

Also, fish is, indeed, a brain food. Recent research suggests that regular intake of omega-3 fatty acids can help treat depression, bipolar disorder, autism, and attention deficit hyperactivity disorder. The right fish can actually make the brain work better.

That's why omega-3-rich fish are prominent in the Anti-Inflammatory Diet and why they are always on the True Food Kitchen menu: wild salmon, steelhead salmon, arctic char, black cod (sablefish), and fresh sardines.

Fish is, however, perhaps the most commonly ruined food on the planet, mostly by overcooking. As the founder of Taoism Lao Tzu said, "Govern a great nation as you would cook a small fish. Do not overdo it." In my experience, people who think they don't like fish have never had really fresh fish properly prepared. We serve some fish raw as sashimi and the rest either pan-seared, grilled, or braised just enough to keep it tender and juicy. At home, I also like to steam fish, which makes it easier to keep the cooking temperature low and even. Blackening fish in a sauté pan or on the grill is not a healthful way to prepare it (or any flesh food); that process generates carcinogenic toxins.

I'm very picky about the kinds of fish I eat and allow on our menu. Grouper, black sea bass, rockfish, and most snapper are endangered from overfishing. Cod, pollock, flounder, halibut, sole, and plaice are still relatively abundant in the Pacific Ocean but seriously depleted in the Atlantic, so I want to know where they come from before deciding. Chilean sea bass and orange roughy are threatened because they do not spawn until they are old—30 years in the case of orange roughy.

Another reason to avoid some fish varieties is contamination with environmental toxins. Fish at the top of the food chain such as shark, swordfish, marlin, and bluefish are the "final stop" for accumulated toxins from all the prey fish they consume; I don't recommend them.

Species that are still abundant and low in toxins include striped bass, wild Alaskan salmon, halibut (especially smaller ones), black cod, herring, sardines, and anchovies, and we feature several of these at True Food. Black cod is a personal favorite, higher in omega-3s than salmon, with a mild buttery flavor and good texture. It is particularly delicious as Miso-Marinated Black Cod (page 132), another of Michael's signature entrées.

Sardines are an excellent choice. Like most small fish, they are low on the food chain and thus extremely low in toxins. Also, overfishing of predator fish has resulted in a doubling of their numbers over the past century, so they are abundant right now. Sardines feed on floating organisms called plankton, an important component of the biodiversity of oceans. Thinning sardine populations isn't just a sustainable practice; it also might even be essential to keeping oceans healthy.

One of my favorite quick and easy lunches is canned sardines (in olive oil; drain off the oil) mashed with Dijon mustard, lemon juice, and chopped onion. I put it on rye crackers or romaine lettuce leaves. If you don't care for these omega-3-rich fish in their canned form, try grilled fresh sardines in good Greek and Italian restaurants (or at our Santa Monica location). If you find them in the market, brush them with olive oil, sprinkle with salt, cook them quickly on a grill or under a broiler, and serve with lemon wedges.

Just don't overcook them! AW

Fresh Tuna–Vegetable Wraps

MAKES 4 SERVINGS

Sprouting does not render grains gluten-free, but many gluten-sensitive people find that baked goods made with sprouted grains are more digestible. They certainly have more flavor. With avocado for healthy fat and quality fresh tuna for protein, this sandwich makes a quick, balanced lunch. AW

SRIRACHA-SESAME SAUCE
Makes ½ cup

- ½ cup mayonnaise
- 2 teaspoons sriracha sauce
- ½ teaspoon dark sesame oil
- ½ teaspoon low-sodium soy sauce

1. Combine all of the Sriracha-Sesame Sauce ingredients in a bowl and whisk well. Cover and refrigerate until needed.

WRAPS

- 2 tablespoons extra-virgin olive oil
- 12 ounces fresh tuna
- 1 teaspoon salt
- 4 sprouted grain tortillas
- 1 small cucumber, sliced
- ½ cup halved grape tomatoes
- 1 avocado, pitted, peeled, and sliced
- 1 cup shredded napa cabbage
- 2 scallions, green part only, sliced on the bias
- 12 sprigs cilantro

2. Preheat the oven to 375°F.

3. Coat tuna with oil and place in a shallow baking dish. Season with the salt and bake for 15 to 20 minutes. Using a fork, flake the fish into large pieces and let cool.

4. Spread each tortilla with 1 tablespoon of the Sriracha-Sesame Sauce and divide the tuna among them, arranging it in the center. Top with the cucumber, tomatoes, avocado, cabbage, scallions, and cilantro. Roll up the tortillas, cut, and serve.

Hemp-Crusted Trout with Thai Broth

MAKES 6 SERVINGS

Hot pots, big simmering vessels that meat, fish, vegetables, and broth are cooked in at the table, come from eastern Asia—China, Japan, and Korea. With this recipe, all the cooking is done beforehand. Each guest is given a bowl with trout and vegetables, then the aromatic stock is poured over the seared fish tableside. You'll surely impress your guests with this theatrical touch. More important, this keeps the fish and broth separate until just the right moment. Look for kabocha squash that are the size of cantaloupe. If you can't find kabocha, substitute butternut squash. MS

THAI BROTH
Makes 6 cups

- 6 cups Dashi (page 238)
- 2 tablespoons chopped fresh ginger
- 2 stalks lemongrass, coarsely chopped
- 5 kaffir lime leaves, torn, or zest of 1 lime
- 2 tablespoons Simple Syrup (see page 242)
- 1 tablespoon fish sauce
- 1 teaspoon sambal oelek or sriracha sauce
  Juice of 1 lime

HEMP SEED CRUST

- 6 tablespoons hemp seeds
- 1 kaffir lime leaf, finely chopped

1. Put the Dashi, ginger, lemongrass, lime leaves, Simple Syrup, and fish sauce in a saucepan. Bring to a simmer over medium heat. Reduce the heat to medium-low and cook for 10 minutes.

2. Remove from the heat and strain the liquid through a fine-mesh strainer into a saucepan, pressing down on the solids to extract all the flavors. Discard the solids in the strainer. Return the broth to low heat and add the sambal oelek. Keep warm until needed. Add the lime juice just before ladling the broth over the vegetables.

3. Pulse 3 tablespoons of the hemp seeds in a spice grinder. Pour into a small bowl and add the remaining 3 tablespoons hemp seeds and lime leaf. Stir to combine. Set aside.

ROASTED OYSTER MUSHROOMS AND KABOCHA SQUASH

- 2 pounds oyster mushrooms, sliced
- 1 kabocha or butternut squash, peeled, seeded, and cut into 1/2-inch wedges
- 3 tablespoons expeller-pressed canola oil
- 1/2 teaspoon salt
  Pinch of freshly ground black pepper

4. Preheat the oven to 400°F. Line a baking sheet with a silicone baking mat or aluminum foil.

5. Place the mushrooms and squash in a large bowl. Add the oil, salt, and pepper, tossing to coat evenly. Arrange the mushrooms and squash in a single layer on the prepared baking sheet. Bake for 20 minutes, until lightly browned and the squash is tender when pierced with a knife.

TROUT

- **6 rainbow or brook trout fillets, skin on**
- **½ teaspoon salt**
- **½ teaspoon freshly ground white pepper**
- **3 to 6 tablespoons expeller-pressed canola oil**
- **2 tablespoons chopped fresh mint**
- **2 tablespoons chopped fresh basil**
- **1 scallion, chopped**
- **3 Thai red chiles, thinly sliced (optional)**

6. Season the trout with the salt and pepper and sprinkle with the hemp seed crust. Heat 3 tablespoons of the canola oil in a nonstick skillet over medium-high heat until the oil shimmers. Add 2 trout fillets to the hot pan, and sear the fish on both sides until golden brown. Transfer to a heated plate and repeat until all the trout is cooked, adding more of the canola oil as needed.

7. To serve, divide the roasted mushrooms and squash among warm serving bowls. Ladle some of the hot Thai broth into each bowl and top with the mint, basil, and scallion. Add a trout fillet to each dish and top with the chiles, if using.

Miso-Marinated Black Cod

This signature True Food Kitchen preparation showcases one of my favorite fish: black cod. A sustainable deep-water species from Alaska, black cod is mild and buttery, with a higher omega-3 content than salmon. I introduced Michael to a similar dish at a New York restaurant and challenged him to come up with his own version for True Food. The dish he created is a best seller at all of our locations, an attractive presentation that is rich and satisfying, yet clean and light at the same time. AW

MISO MARINADE
Makes 1½ cups

½ cup mirin

½ cup white (*shiro*) miso

½ cup evaporated cane sugar

1. Whisk together all of the Miso Marinade ingredients and refrigerate until ready to use.

COD AND VEGETABLES

4   (5- to 6-ounce) black cod fillets

1   cup Dashi (page 238)

8   heads baby bok choy, halved

1   cup Roasted Mushrooms (page 242)

2. Arrange the fish in a single layer in a shallow baking pan. Using your hands, rub the Miso Marinade all over each piece of fish. Wash your hands. Let the fish marinate for at least 30 minutes and up to 12 hours in the refrigerator.

3. Preheat the oven to broil.

4. Remove the fish from the refrigerator and pour ½ cup of the Dashi into the baking pan. Broil the fish for 10 to 15 minutes, depending on the desired doneness. The fish will continue to cook once removed from the broiler.

5. While the fish is cooking, place the bok choy halves in a skillet, and add the remaining ½ cup Dashi. Cover and steam over medium-high heat until cooked but still crunchy, about 3 minutes. Add the Roasted Mushrooms and heat them through. Place the vegetables and broth in heated bowls. Add the cod and serve.

Halibut with Fingerling Potatoes and Umami Sauce

MAKES 4 SERVINGS

Halibut is a delicate fish that is easy to cook under the broiler, a method that seals the surface and renders it moist and flaky. Alaskan halibut is in season through spring and summer, and Seafood Watch rates it highly for sustainability. Umami Sauce and wok-style vegetables complement halibut's light, gentle flavor. If you can't find Brussels sprouts, you may substitute a pound of asparagus, cut into 1-inch pieces. MS

1   **pound fingerling potatoes, cubed**

1   **tablespoon extra-virgin olive oil**

     Salt and freshly ground black pepper

1   **pound Brussels sprouts, cut in quarters**

4   **(5- to 6-ounce) halibut steaks**

1½ **teaspoons salt**

2   **tablespoons expeller-pressed canola oil**

3   **cups Roasted Mushrooms (page 242)**

1   **tablespoon Wok Aromatics (page 237)**

½   **cup Umami Sauce (page 236)**

1. Preheat the oven to 400°F. Line a baking sheet with aluminum foil.

2. Arrange the potato cubes on the prepared baking sheet and toss them with the olive oil, salt, and pepper. Roast for 25 minutes, or until tender when pierced with a knife. Remove from the oven and set aside. Preheat the oven to broil.

3. Bring a large pot of water to a boil. Fill a large bowl with ice cubes and cold water.

4. Plunge the quartered Brussels sprouts into the boiling water for 2 minutes. Using a slotted spoon, transfer them from the hot water to the ice bath for 3 minutes. The cold water allows the sprouts to keep their bright green color. Drain them in a colander.

5. Pat the halibut steaks dry with a paper towel and season with the salt. Heat an ovenproof skillet large enough to hold the fish in a single layer over medium-high heat. When the pan is hot, heat 1 tablespoon of the canola oil until it shimmers. Put the fish in the hot pan and immediately place under the broiler. Cook until golden brown or to the preferred doneness, 8 to 10 minutes.

6. Heat another skillet over medium-high heat. Add the remaining 1 tablespoon canola oil and heat until it shimmers, but do not let it smoke. Add the potatoes and cook until crisp. Stir in the Roasted Mushrooms, Brussels sprouts, and Wok Aromatics. Add 1 tablespoon water and cook until hot and the water evaporates. Add 2 tablespoons of the Umami Sauce and toss to coat.

7. To serve, divide the potato-mushroom mixture among warmed plates. Top each with a piece of roasted halibut and drizzle on some of the remaining Umami Sauce. Serve with any remaining Umami Sauce on the side.

Tomato-Braised Tuna

Family meal in a restaurant kitchen is the time when all the chefs, cooks, and service staff get together to eat and strategize before the restaurant opens to the public. It's the perfect opportunity for a chef to try out new ideas and get feedback on a dish—sometimes for weeks—from the staff. This dish was a hit with everyone. MS

3 tablespoons extra-virgin olive oil

1 medium onion, diced

1 small fennel bulb, diced

2 garlic cloves, mashed

1 small Fresno chile, minced

1 small jalapeño chile, minced

1⅛ teaspoons salt

½ cup dry white wine

⅛ teaspoon saffron

1 (28-ounce) can pureed San Marzano tomatoes

6 ounces boiling potatoes, such as red bliss, cubed

1 teaspoon fennel seeds

½ teaspoon freshly ground white pepper

12 ounces ahi tuna, cut into 1½-inch cubes

¼ cup pitted and slivered green olives, such as Picholine or Castelvetrano

1 teaspoon freshly grated lemon zest

1 tablespoon freshly squeezed lemon juice

1 scallion, chopped

1. In a large pot, heat 2 tablespoons of the olive oil over medium-high heat. Add the onion and fennel and sauté for 2 minutes. Add the garlic and sauté for an additional minute. Add the chiles. Season with ⅛ teaspoon of the salt and continue to cook for another minute. Add the wine and saffron and deglaze the pan, stirring all the vegetables and reducing the sauce for just 2 minutes. Add the pureed tomatoes, potatoes, fennel seeds, 1 cup water, remaining 1 teaspoon salt, and the white pepper. Bring to a simmer and cook until the potatoes are not quite done. Stir in the tuna and continue to cook until the potatoes and tuna are cooked. Fold in the olives, lemon zest, and lemon juice. Taste and adjust the seasonings.

2. Serve in warmed bowls garnished with the scallions and drizzled with the remaining 1 tablespoon olive oil.

Embracing the Bison

I haven't had any beef since I stopped eating meat forty years ago. Of all the animal foods in the mainstream American diet, beef is the least healthy, both for individuals and the planet. My intention was to have no beef on our menu, but Sam was insistent that you can't run a successful restaurant without it. He suggested steak tacos made with a modest amount of grass-fed beef. From the first, it was one of our most popular items.

But I was never really comfortable with having beef on the menu, so I asked Michael to look into the possibility of using bison, or American buffalo. Bison meat contains about one-third the fat and two-thirds the calories of a similar portion of beef. Nearly extinct by the 1880s after a century of mass slaughter, bison now number more than 500,000 and are raised on large commercial ranches throughout the United States. Only some of it is grass fed and free of antibiotics and growth-promoting hormones. Michael found a vendor who could promise us a good supply of the quality we require.

The next step was to decide what to make with it. Bison meat can taste gamey if it is not well prepared, and overcooking ruins it. A burger seemed like the best bet. Michael realized that he could balance bison's sharp, aggressively "wild" flavor with multiple mellow, savory notes, so he created Umami Sauce (page 236) from soy sauce, vinegar, garlic, and nutritional yeast flakes and mixed it into the ground meat. That kept it juicy as well, and with toppings of caramelized onions, shiitake mushrooms, and shaved Parmesan, the bison burger turned out to deliver "a real symphony of flavors, just extraordinary," Michael says.

One last crucial test remained. "Sam is the best burger critic I know," says Michael. "He has eaten every kind you can imagine and has an amazing ability to know what will work with the public."

"It was the best burger I'd ever eaten," recalls Sam.

Sure enough, our Bison Umami Burger (page 140) was an instant hit, and it remains one of our top sellers. AW

Bison Umami Burger

On a burger tour of Los Angeles, Sam and I must have sampled about twenty burgers in two days. The standout was at Umami Burger, in Hollywood. The unique umami flavors of Parmesan and roasted shiitakes enhanced the burger's meatiness. Back in our Phoenix test kitchen, I took it a step further by adding nutritional yeast flakes to the ground bison and a dash of our own Umami Sauce. MS

2¼ pounds ground bison

2 tablespoons plus 1½ teaspoons nutritional yeast flakes

1½ teaspoons salt

½ teaspoon freshly ground black pepper

1 cup Roasted Mushrooms (page 242)

1 cup Caramelized Onions (page 240)

6 flax seed buns

⅓ cup Umami Sauce (page 236), warmed

⅓ cup grated Parmigiano-Reggiano cheese

1. Using your hands, mix the bison, yeast flakes, salt, and pepper in a bowl to combine. Divide the meat into 6 patties. Wash your hands.

2. Preheat the grill to medium-high heat. Preheat the oven to 400°F if the Roasted Mushrooms and Caramelized Onions were prepared in advance and cooled. Put them in a baking dish and place in the oven to warm while the burgers are cooking.

3. Grill the burgers for 5 to 7 minutes per side, depending on the desired degree of doneness. Toast the buns.

4. Place the burgers on the buns. Top with the mushrooms and onions and drizzle each one with a bit of the Umami Sauce. Sprinkle on the cheese and serve.

Chicken Teriyaki

MAKES 4 SERVINGS

This was the first dish I created when we started developing the True Food Kitchen menu, and it is our most popular entrée at every location. It's a perfect example of how True Food breaks with traditional restaurants—most places put about 3 ounces of vegetables in this dish; we use 8 ounces. To keep your wok or skillet from cooling down when cooking, make this in two quick, stir-fried batches. MS

BROWN RICE

- 1   **cup brown rice**
- 1   **tablespoon extra-virgin olive oil**
- 1   **teaspoon salt**

CHICKEN AND VEGETABLES

- 2   **tablespoons expeller-pressed canola oil**
- 1   **pound boneless, skinless chicken breasts, sliced into 1/4-inch pieces**
- 2   **tablespoons Wok Aromatics (page 237)**
- 4   **heads baby bok choy, cut in half**
- 2   **cups broccoli florets**
- 4   **ounces green beans, stemmed, strings removed, and cut into 1/2-inch pieces**
- 4   **ounces sugar snap peas, stemmed and strings removed**
- 1   **medium onion, thinly sliced**
- 1/2   **cup Teriyaki Sauce (page 235)**
- 1   **avocado, pitted, peeled, and sliced**
- 1   **tablespoon toasted sesame seeds**

1. Combine the rice, 2 cups water, oil, and salt in a saucepan with a tight-fitting lid. Place over medium-high heat and bring to a boil. Stir and cover. Reduce the heat to a simmer and cook for 50 minutes.

2. Heat a wok or skillet over medium-high heat. Add 1 tablespoon of the canola oil and heat until it shimmers. Add half of the chicken and stir-fry until it turns golden brown. Add 1 tablespoon of the Wok Aromatics and half of the bok choy, broccoli, beans, sugar snap peas, and onion. Cook, stirring constantly, until the vegetables are crisp-tender and the chicken is cooked through, 5 to 7 minutes. Add 1/4 cup of the Teriyaki Sauce and stir-fry to combine. Divide the chicken, vegetables, and sauce between two warm bowls on top of some brown rice.

3. Remove the wok or skillet from the heat and carefully wipe out with a paper towel. Repeat the directions for making the second batch of chicken and vegetables.

4. Garnish with sliced avocado and sesame seeds before serving.

Turkey Bolognese

Whether you use gluten-free pasta, which takes a few minutes longer to cook, or wheat pasta, top it with this lean turkey sauce. This is True Food comfort food at its best. MS

1 teaspoon extra-virgin olive oil

1 carrot, diced

2 ounces shiitake mushrooms, stemmed and diced

3 garlic cloves, minced

1 small onion, diced

1 pound ground turkey

½ teaspoon salt

1 (14-ounce) can chopped San Marzano tomatoes, with juice

3 or 4 sprigs thyme

Pinch of red pepper flakes

1 pound tagliatelle or fettuccine

2 tablespoons chopped fresh Italian parsley

2 tablespoons chopped fresh basil

Grated Parmigiano-Reggiano cheese, for serving

1. Heat the olive oil over medium-high heat in a saucepan and add the carrot and mushrooms. Sauté, stirring frequently, until they begin to caramelize, about 10 minutes, then add the garlic and onion. Sauté until the onions are translucent, about 5 minutes. Add the ground turkey and season with the salt. Cook, stirring occasionally, until the turkey loses its pink color, about 5 minutes more. Add the tomatoes and bring to a simmer. Add the thyme and red pepper and cook over low heat for 20 minutes.

2. While the sauce is cooking, bring a large pot of salted water to a boil. Add the pasta and cook until al dente, according to the package directions. Pour through a colander to drain. Divide the pasta among serving bowls and top with the sauce, parsley, and basil. Serve with grated cheese on the side.

Chicken, Corn, and Black Bean Enchiladas with Tomatillo Salsa

MAKES 4 TO 6 SERVINGS

I like to cook Mexican food at home, and I love to go out to quality Sonoran restaurants. But they are hard to find, even in Phoenix; Mexican restaurant food is piled with excessive cheese and warmed into goo on steam tables for hours on end. These enchiladas are based on traditional, fresh ingredients (with our usual international twist) and leave the fatty excesses behind. I use a smaller amount of a full-flavored cheese like Spanish Manchego to ramp up the flavor. This dish is really all about the vegetables and the picante bite of the salsa. MS

TOMATILLO SALSA

Makes 2 cups

6   **medium fresh tomatillos, papery skins removed and quartered**

1   **small onion, quartered**

¼   **cup Chicken Stock (page 237) or water**

2   **teaspoons champagne vinegar**

2   **teaspoons extra-virgin olive oil**

    Juice of 1 lime

2   **tablespoons fresh cilantro**

1   **teaspoon dried whole oregano leaves**

½   **teaspoon ground cumin**

½   **teaspoon red pepper flakes**

1. Place all of the Tomatillo Salsa ingredients in a food processor or blender and blend until smooth. Leftover salsa may be stored in the refrigerator for up to 3 days.

Continues»

ENCHILADAS

2   cups corn kernels, from
     2 ears corn

1½   cups diced roasted
     chicken

1   (4-ounce) jicama, peeled
     and diced

1   poblano chile, roasted,
     seeded, and diced

1   small zucchini, diced

⅓   cup cooked black beans

3   ounces Manchego cheese,
     diced

¼   teaspoon chili powder

     Salt and freshly ground
     black pepper

6   (6-inch) corn tortillas

½   cup shredded Manchego
     cheese

6   tablespoons Greek-style
     plain yogurt

2   teaspoons chopped fresh
     cilantro

6   lime wedges

2. Place the corn kernels in a large skillet over medium-high heat. Cook, stirring occasionally, until lightly browned.

3. Preheat the oven to 350°F.

4. In a mixing bowl, combine the chicken, jicama, chile, zucchini, black beans, diced Manchego, and chili powder. Mix well and add salt and pepper as needed.

5. Ladle ¼ cup of the Tomatillo Salsa into a shallow, ovenproof baking dish large enough to hold 6 enchiladas in a single layer.

6. Arrange the tortillas on a flat surface. Spoon the filling into the center of the tortillas. Roll the tortillas around the filling and place them seam side down in the baking dish. Nestle the enchiladas against one another to help them hold their shape. Top with ¾ cup of the salsa and the shredded Manchego. Bake until hot, about 30 minutes.

7. Serve with dollops of yogurt, the cilantro sprinkled on top, and the lime wedges on the side.

Bento

The traditional Japanese bento box is a compartmentalized container that typically contains fish or meat, rice, vegetables, and pickles. Ordering a bento box in a Japanese restaurant allows you try many different preparations. Our version—and you don't need an actual bento box—is composed of some hot and some cold dishes that can for the most part be served alone, but together they make a visually stunning and satisfying meal. If you don't own bento boxes, this looks just as beautiful on plates and in small bowls.

Furikake is a condiment of chopped nori and black and white sesame seeds that is used in Japan for sprinkling on rice and other dishes. Kimchee is a Korean condiment of fermented vegetables, including napa cabbage. Burdock root is a popular root vegetable in Japan. All are available in Asian markets and many supermarkets. MS

GLAZED BURDOCK ROOT

- 8 ounces burdock root
- 1 dried Thai or other hot chile
- 1 tablespoon expeller-pressed canola oil
- 3 tablespoons sake
- 1½ teaspoons evaporated cane sugar
- 1 tablespoon mirin
- 1 tablespoon low-sodium soy sauce

1. Scrub the burdock root under running water but do not scrape the skin off. Cut into matchstick-size pieces.

2. Soak the chile in warm water for 2 minutes, until soft. Cut off the stem end and remove the seeds. Slice into thin rounds.

3. Add the oil to a skillet and heat over high heat. Add the burdock root and stir-fry, coating it thoroughly with the oil. Stir in the chile and mix well. Lower the heat to medium and add the sake, sugar, mirin, and soy sauce, tossing to combine all the ingredients. Cook until most of the liquid in the pan is gone. Transfer the burdock to a plate to cool.

BROWN RICE

- 1 cup brown rice
- 1 tablespoon extra-virgin olive oil
- 1 teaspoon salt

4. Combine the rice, 2 cups water, oil, and salt in a saucepan with a tight-fitting lid. Place over medium-high heat and bring to a boil. Stir and cover. Reduce the heat to a simmer and cook for 50 minutes.

5. Remove the pot from the heat and let stand, covered, for 10 minutes. Fluff the rice with a fork and adjust the seasonings. Keep covered until ready to assemble.

Continues »

SPINACH

2 teaspoons expeller-pressed canola oil

4 to 5 ounces spinach leaves

¼ cup Citrus-Sesame Sauce (page 235)

1 tablespoon toasted sesame seeds

6. Heat a skillet or wok over high heat. Add the oil and, when it shimmers, add the spinach and quickly stir-fry. Add 1½ teaspoons water and toss. Add the Citrus-Sesame Sauce and toss to coat. Place on a serving plate and finish with the toasted sesame seeds.

GRILLED SHRIMP

16 large shrimp, peeled and deveined

16 fresh green shiso, mint, or basil leaves

16 honshimeji mushrooms

½ cup Asian Barbecue Sauce (page 234)

7. If using bamboo skewers, soak them in water for 20 minutes. Preheat the grill.

8. Wrap each shrimp with a shiso leaf and pierce with a skewer to hold in place. Add a honshimeji mushroom to each skewer. Baste with the Asian Barbecue Sauce and grill for 45 seconds to 1 minute on each side, until done.

TO ASSEMBLE

⅓ cup *furikake*

1 cup kimchee

9. To compose the bento plates, portion the rice into bento box compartments or into small bowls and top with the *furikake*. If serving on plates instead of in bento boxes, place the rice bowls on each plate. Place the shrimp skewers in another compartment or on a section of the serving plates. Divide the kimchee, spinach, and burdock root among the compartments or the plates. Serve immediately.

Glazed Burdock Root

Kim Chee

Grilled Shrimp

Spinach

Brown Rice

Bibimbap

Bibimbap, *Korean for "mixed meal," is usually made with rice topped with meats, seafood, vegetables (pickled or otherwise), and a fried egg. Our version is served with rice noodles topped with various in-season vegetables and homemade pickles. I like to experiment with different vegetables, often adding shrimp or tofu pieces to the mix.* Bibimbap *is traditionally served with ingredients laid out in a decorative pattern. Once served, each person adds spicy* gochujang, *Korean chile paste.* Gochujang *and pickled daikon can be found in Asian markets.* MS

KOREAN BROTH

Makes about 6 cups

- 6 cups Dashi (page 238)
- 2 tablespoons low-sodium soy sauce
- 2 tablespoons mirin
- 6 garlic cloves, mashed
- 1½ teaspoons Korean chile paste (*gochujang*)
- 2 tablespoons hoisin sauce
- 1½ teaspoons grated fresh ginger
- 1½ teaspoons dark sesame oil

1. In a saucepan, combine the Dashi, soy sauce, mirin, garlic, Korean chile paste, hoisin, and ginger. Bring to a simmer over medium heat. Reduce the heat to low, and simmer for 20 minutes. Stir in the sesame oil. Remove from the heat and keep warm, or cover and refrigerate until ready to use. Reheat the broth when assembling the dish.

MARINATED DAIKON

- 2 teaspoons *gochugaru* (Korean red chile powder) or other hot pure chile powder
- ½ cup Dashi (page 238)
- 1 package pickled daikon, shredded

2. Combine the chile powder and Dashi in a small saucepan and cook over medium heat for 2 minutes to let the flavors infuse. Let cool, and then add the daikon. Let marinate for 20 minutes, and then remove the daikon. Set the daikon aside and discard the liquid.

PICKLED CARROTS

Makes about 1 cup

- 2 teaspoons unseasoned rice wine vinegar
- 1 teaspoon salt
- 1 large carrot, cut into matchsticks

3. In a small saucepan over medium-high heat, combine the vinegar, salt, and 1 cup water. Bring to a boil and pour over the carrots in a heat-proof bowl. Let cool, and then remove the carrots from the liquid. Discard the liquid.

Continues »

SAUTÉED MUSHROOMS WITH GINGER AND GARLIC

1 tablespoon expeller-pressed canola oil

¼ teaspoon dark sesame oil

4 ounces shiitake mushrooms, stemmed and sliced

2 ounces oyster mushrooms, sliced

2 ounces maitake mushrooms, sliced

½ teaspoon grated fresh ginger

1 garlic clove, mashed

¼ teaspoon salt

Pinch of freshly ground black pepper

½ teaspoon low-sodium soy sauce

4. Heat a nonstick skillet over medium heat. Add the oils and, when they begin to shimmer, add the shiitake mushrooms. Sauté until softened, then add the oyster and maitake mushrooms. Sauté until the mushrooms are golden brown, about 10 minutes. Add the ginger and garlic, season with the salt and pepper, and cook for another minute. Stir in the soy sauce. Remove the pan from the heat.

NOODLES, SHRIMP, AND VEGETABLES

4 ounces green beans, stemmed and strings removed

8 ounces rice stick noodles

3 scallions, thinly sliced lengthwise

3 cups cooked shrimp (boiled or grilled)

½ cup watercress

¼ cup toasted nori strips, about 1 by ¼ inch

1 cup fresh bean sprouts

¼ cup hoisin sauce

2 tablespoons Korean chile paste (*gochujang*)

5. Bring a large pot of salted water to a boil. Fill a large bowl with ice cubes and cold water.

6. Plunge the green beans into the boiling water for 2 to 3 minutes, until crisp-tender. Using tongs or a slotted spoon, transfer the beans to the ice bath for 3 minutes. Drain through a colander. Cut into 2-inch lengths.

7. Add the rice stick noodles and green beans to the reheated Korean Broth. Divide among bowls.

8. Working clockwise in a circle, portion the Sautéed Mushrooms with Ginger and Garlic, Pickled Carrots, Marinated Daikon, scallion threads, shrimp, and watercress on top of the noodles. Sprinkle with the nori strips and finish with a pinch of bean sprouts in the center. Serve with the hoisin sauce and Korean chile paste on the side so that each diner may add them according to taste.

PASTA & NOODLES

Pasta is comfort food. It can also be healthy food if you take a few precautions. Buy high-quality pasta and do not overcook it. Its glycemic load (impact on blood sugar) is less if it is chewy, not mushy. Do not serve huge portions. And put it in highly flavored Asian broths or low-fat sauces with plenty of vegetables. Try Italian pasta made from spelt, Thai rice stick noodles, and Japanese ultra-low-carb yam noodles (shirataki). Even gluten-free varieties of pasta are now available. AW

Spaghetti with Bottarga

Bottarga di muggine *is the cured roe sacs of the gray mullet, an important food fish of the Mediterranean and a traditional Italian delicacy (do not confuse it with the much saltier and fishier* bottarga di tonno, *from tuna). Sometimes referred to as "poor man's caviar," bottarga is high in omega-3 fatty acids and has a rich, buttery taste. If you can't find it locally, a 4-ounce package can be purchased from buonitalia.com. Just before the pasta is served, the grated bottarga is sprinkled on top.* AW

1	(4-ounce) package *bottarga di muggine*
1	pound spaghetti
½	cup extra-virgin olive oil
⅓	cup minced garlic
½	teaspoon red pepper flakes, plus more for serving
¼	teaspoon salt
1½	cups chopped fresh Italian parsley

1. Peel the membrane from the bottarga with a sharp knife. If you cannot get it all, just start to grate the bottarga and remove the membrane as you go. Grate the bottarga as you would Parmesan; a rasp grater or the fine side of a box grater works well. Set aside.

2. Bring a large pot of salted water to a boil. Add the spaghetti and cook until al dente, according to the package directions. Have warmed pasta bowls ready to serve.

3. While the spaghetti is cooking, heat the oil in a large skillet over medium-high heat. When hot, add the garlic, red pepper flakes, and salt. Stir and cook for 1 minute. Add the parsley and continue cooking just until the parsley is bright green, 1 to 2 minutes more. Remove from the heat.

4. Just before the spaghetti is cooked, remove 2 tablespoons of the pasta water and stir it into the parsley mixture. Drain the pasta in a colander and add it to the parsley mixture in the skillet. Toss well, adjust the seasonings, and divide among the warm bowls.

5. Top each bowl with a generous amount of the grated bottarga and serve immediately with additional red pepper flakes on the side.

Fettuccine with Kale Pesto

Unlike pesto made with basil, this kale version doesn't lose its bright green color, and it has more micronutrients and protective phytonutrients. Kale pesto is also delicious, and people who try it can't believe it contains no basil. Keep it on hand in the freezer and dinner will be ready in the time it takes for the pasta to cook. AW

1   **pound fettuccine or pappardelle**

1   **cup Kale Pesto (page 234)**

1   **cup grated Parmigiano-Reggiano cheese, plus more for serving**

1.   Bring a large pot of salted water to a boil. Add the fettuccine and cook until al dente, according to the package directions.

2.   Just before the pasta is done, remove 2 tablespoons of the pasta water and add it to the Kale Pesto. Add the cheese and mix well.

3.   Drain the pasta and toss with the pesto mixture. Serve with extra cheese for those who might want it.

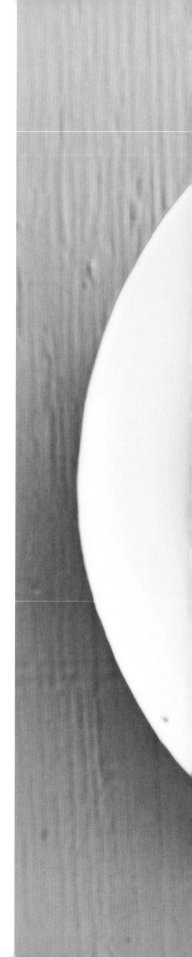

The Problem of Proper Portions

The Internet has changed the restaurant business dramatically—for the better, I think. These days, there's no need to guess about your customers' opinions. On sites like Urbanspoon and especially Yelp, feedback has been immediate and passionate; for example: "Woop! Yay for TF's super-chic patio, interesting drinks, and AWESOME healthy food options! I love it!"

But interspersed among the raves, we do get— infrequently, fortunately—negative comments. Most commonly, these express disappointment over the relatively modest size of our portions; "ridiculously small" typifies this sentiment.

Are such critiques warranted?

Before we opened, Sam and I had many discussions about proper portion size. Sam understands the modern American restaurant business and the fact that serving sizes have been relentlessly ratcheted up over the past couple of decades. He worried that the sensible, healthy portions I favored would seem paltry.

But I pointed out that our motto, "Globally Inspired Cuisine," should refer not only to *what* we serve, but also to *how much*. I told him that on a recent visit to Tuscany, I had been dished up a vast mound of pasta because "that's how much Americans eat." I was embarrassed for my country and insisted upon receiving just the typical Italian portion, which would easily fit in a teacup. The

experience stayed with me. Clearly someone somewhere in American food culture needed to strike a blow for realistic portion sizes.

That someone is us. Our appetizers, such as the edamame dumplings, are just that: a few bites to stimulate the appetite, not meals in themselves. Our entrées are satisfying, but the Tofu Curry with Cauliflower, Rice Noodles, and Cashews (page 167) is no more nor less than one would receive in a quality Bangkok restaurant; in other words, just enough.

Increasingly, we seem to be bringing the Yelpers along—or, more likely, the moderate majority was simply waiting for the complaints to reach critical mass. Whatever the reason, I've noticed that in recent months, there are more and more customers lining up on our side, attesting that the portions "are not over the top" and leave the customer "satisfied without being uncomfortable."

Thank you, Internet. I could not have said it better myself. AW

Spaghetti with Tuna Puttanesca

MAKES 4 SERVINGS

Puttanesca is a Southern Italian tomato sauce flavored with anchovies, garlic, capers, and hot red pepper flakes. This version incorporates chunks of pan-seared fresh ahi tuna. Try it with spaghetti and garnish with a generous sprinkling of chopped herbs—parsley, basil, and oregano—for color contrast. AW

½ cup pitted Kalamata olives

2 tablespoons capers, rinsed

3 garlic cloves, mashed

2 or 3 anchovy fillets

1 teaspoon red pepper flakes (or more to taste)

¼ cup extra-virgin olive oil

1 pound spaghetti

4 (3-ounce) pieces ahi tuna, diced

2 cups Tomato Sauce (page 236)

¼ cup chopped mixed fresh basil, oregano, and Italian parsley

¼ cup grated Parmigiano-Reggiano cheese

1. Put the olives, capers, garlic, anchovies, red pepper flakes, and 2 tablespoons of the olive oil in a food processor. Pulse just until coarsely mixed. Transfer to a bowl, cover, and set aside.

2. Bring a large pot of salted water to a boil. Add the spaghetti and cook until al dente, according to the package directions. Pour through a colander to drain.

3. While the spaghetti is cooking, heat the remaining 2 tablespoons olive oil in a large pot until it shimmers. Add the olive-caper mixture and the tuna. Sauté for 2 to 3 minutes, until the tuna just begins to lose its pink color. Add the tomato sauce to the tuna and cook until heated through. Add the spaghetti to the pot and toss to coat with the sauce. Divide among warm pasta bowls and garnish with the chopped herbs and cheese before serving.

Corn-Ricotta Ravioli

MAKES ABOUT 30 TORTELLINI; 4 TO 6 SERVINGS

Filling ravioli with corn is unusual, but the pure, buttery sweetness and crunch of the kernels inside the pasta work well. Use a high-quality, whole-milk ricotta cheese that has been drained overnight in a coffee filter–lined colander to remove excess moisture from the cheese. This will keep the filling firm. You can make your own pasta dough or purchase fresh sheets in many markets. MS

PASTA DOUGH

1   cup all-purpose flour

1   cup high-gluten flour

2   large eggs

1. Place the flours in a large bowl and form a well in the center. In a small bowl, whisk together the eggs with 2 tablespoons cold water. Add the egg-water mixture to the center of the well. Using a fork, stir the wet mixture into the dry mixture, using a circular motion to combine. Turn the dough out onto a clean, floured work surface. Knead for 4 to 5 minutes, and then shape into a smooth, elastic ball. Cover the dough with plastic wrap and let rest for 30 minutes before making the ravioli.

PARMESAN-CORN BROTH

3   ears corn

2   tablespoons extra-virgin olive oil

$\frac{1}{3}$ cup grated Parmigiano-Reggiano

1   teaspoon agave nectar

2   teaspoons salt

2. Slice the kernels off the cobs and place in a saucepan. Holding the cobs over the saucepan, scrape the cobs with the back of a knife to squeeze out all the corn milk. Cut the cobs in half and add them to the saucepan along with 2½ cups water. Simmer for 20 minutes over medium heat. Remove from the heat and, using tongs, fish out and discard the cobs. Let cool for 10 minutes, then put the corn and liquid in a blender along with the cheese, agave, and salt. Blend until smooth. Pour the broth through a fine-mesh strainer back into the saucepan; discard the solids. Keep warm until needed.

CORN-RICOTTA FILLING

½   teaspoon extra-virgin olive oil

1   small garlic clove, minced

1½   cups corn kernels, scraped from 2 ears of corn

1   teaspoon salt

   Pinch of cayenne pepper

1   cup fresh ricotta cheese, drained through cheesecloth overnight in the refrigerator

6   ounces mozzarella cheese, grated

2   teaspoons freshly grated lime zest

2   teaspoons freshly squeezed lime juice

3. Heat the olive oil in a large saucepan over medium heat. Add the garlic and 1 cup of the corn kernels (reserve the rest for finishing the dish) and cook, stirring constantly, for about 5 minutes, or until lightly browned. Add the salt,

Continues »

cayenne, and 1 teaspoon water. Lower the heat and simmer until the water has evaporated and the corn is cooked. Remove from the heat and let cool for 10 minutes. Put the corn mixture in a blender and blend until smooth. Transfer to a bowl.

4. Stir in the ricotta, mozzarella, lime zest, and lime juice. Mix well and taste to see if the filling needs more salt and pepper. Set aside.

RAVIOLI AND TOPPING

All-purpose flour, for dusting

3 **ounces (about 2 cups) spinach leaves**

1 **cup Oven-Roasted Tomatoes (page 240)**

¼ **cup grated Parmigiano-Reggiano cheese**

2 **tablespoons chopped fresh Italian parsley**

2 **tablespoons chopped fresh basil**

5. Cut the dough into 2 pieces. If using a pasta machine, set the machine on the thickest setting, and roll out one piece of dough. Fold it over and roll it out again, on progressively thinner settings, until it is roughly $\frac{1}{16}$ inch thick. Repeat with the remaining piece of dough. If don't have a pasta machine, roll the dough as thinly as possible using a floured rolling pin.

6. To make the ravioli, have a bowl of water and a pastry brush at your workspace. Dust a baking sheet lightly with flour to hold the completed ravioli. Dust the work surface with flour and lay out one pasta sheet. Using a 2-inch biscuit cutter, cut 12 to 16 circles. Brush each one lightly with water and then place about 1 table-spoon of the Corn-Ricotta Filling in the center of half of the rounds. Cover each one with the remaining pasta rounds. To seal, press the pasta firmly down around the filling with your fingers, working out from the edge of the filling, to press out any air that may be trapped. Place the ravioli onto the prepared baking sheet. Repeat the process until all the ravioli are completed.

7. Bring a large pot of salted water to a boil. Lower the heat to a simmer, gently lower the ravioli into the water, and cook for 4 to 5 minutes. Simmering, rather than boiling, the ravioli will keep them from coming apart while cooking. Using a slotted spoon, transfer the cooked ravioli to warm serving bowls.

8. While the pasta is cooking, place the remaining $\frac{1}{2}$ cup corn kernels in a large skillet over medium-high heat. Cook them, stirring occasionally, until lightly browned. Add the spinach, Parmesan-Corn Broth, and Oven-Roasted Tomatoes and cook, stirring regularly, until hot and the spinach wilts. Top the ravioli with the vegetables, broth, cheese, parsley, and basil before serving.

Tofu Curry with Cauliflower, Rice Noodles, and Cashews

MAKES 4 TO 6 SERVINGS

Coconut water is blended with coconut cream for a velvety, rich curry sauce. A modest amount of curry powder, along with Thai red curry paste (available in many supermarkets) and other top-quality aromatics, balances the dish. Fresh vegetables are added near the end, and cooked only until just tender. MS

CURRY BROTH

$2^2/_3$ cups unsweetened coconut cream

$1^2/_3$ cups unsweetened coconut water

1   lemongrass stalk, mashed

1   tablespoon plus $1^1/_2$ teaspoons chopped fresh ginger

2   dried shiitake mushroom caps

3   tablespoons Thai red curry paste

2   tablespoons honey

1   tablespoon freshly squeezed lime juice

1   kaffir lime leaf, torn, or 1 teaspoon freshly grated lime zest

4   sprigs cilantro

3   fresh basil leaves

$1/_3$ teaspoon curry powder

$1/_8$ teaspoon salt

NOODLES, TOFU, AND VEGETABLES

1   small boiling potato, such as red bliss, diced

12   ounces extra-firm tofu, cut into large squares

3   ounces shiitake mushrooms, stemmed and sliced

1   small onion, thinly sliced

$1^1/_2$ cups cauliflower florets

2   carrots, sliced on the bias

3   ounces sugar snap peas, trimmed

     Salt

1   (8-ounce) package rice stick noodles, soaked according to package directions

$1/_2$ cup chopped roasted unsalted cashews

$1/_4$ cup fresh cilantro leaves

1. Combine all of the Curry Broth ingredients in a large pot over medium heat. Once the broth starts to simmer, reduce the heat to low and cook for 30 minutes. Do not boil. Strain the broth through a fine-mesh strainer into a large saucepan. Set aside. (The broth may be made ahead and refrigerated for 3 days or frozen for up to 1 month.)

2. Put the potato in the Curry Broth and cook over medium heat, but do not boil, just until the pieces start to become tender when pierced with a fork. Add the tofu, mushrooms, onion, cauliflower, and carrots. Continue to cook until all the vegetables are tender, about 5 minutes. Add the sugar snap peas and cook for another 2 minutes. Adjust the seasoning with salt.

3. Divide the curry among warm bowls, then add the noodles to the bowls. Top with the cashews and cilantro before serving.

VEGETABLES

I've come to like every vegetable I hated as a kid—the result of having them fresh and well prepared. Vegetables are a main component of the Anti-Inflammatory Diet because they are the best source of health-protective phytonutrients. Vegetables of all colors accompany appetizers and main courses at True Food Kitchen, and we also serve them up as sides. AW

Asian Cauliflower

If you find cauliflower boring, try this flavorful, visually striking Asian dish. Don't overcook the cauliflower; it should have a bit of crunch. This is a perfect complement to curries or Asian noodles. If you want a spicy dish, add thinly sliced chile peppers with the shallots and garlic and serve with sriracha. If fresh tomatoes aren't in season, use 1 cup of diced canned tomatoes, drained. AW

1 tablespoon expeller-pressed canola oil

2 shallots, thinly sliced

3 garlic cloves, minced

2 tablespoons low-sodium soy sauce

3 tomatoes, peeled, seeded, and diced

1 large head cauliflower, cut into florets

1 small onion, thinly sliced

⅔ cup Mushroom Stock (page 238)

½ teaspoon freshly squeezed lemon juice

2 teaspoons evaporated cane sugar

2 scallions, thinly sliced

½ cup chopped fresh cilantro

1. Heat the oil in a skillet over medium heat. Add the shallots and garlic and sauté for 1 minute. Add the soy sauce and tomatoes and cook for another 3 minutes. Add the cauliflower, onion, Mushroom Stock, lemon juice, sugar, and scallions. Reduce the heat and cook, stirring frequently, until the cauliflower is tender but still crisp, about 10 minutes. Add 2 tablespoons water as it cooks to prevent sticking, if necessary. Do not overcook.

2. Transfer the cauliflower to a bowl and sprinkle with the cilantro before serving.

Stir-Fried Long Beans with Citrus-Sesame Sauce

MAKES 4 TO 6 SERVINGS

Common in Asian dishes including stir-fries and omelets, long-podded beans—sometimes reaching a foot or more in length—are finding their way from farmers' markets and Asian markets onto menus and into home kitchens. Southern Arizona desert gardeners like Andy know these beans well, as they are among the few vegetables that thrive in blast-furnace summer heat. Long beans have a dry flesh that lends itself to panfrying or wok cooking. The tahini and lemon give this dish a bright flavor that complements baked fish or roasted poultry. Make sure the beans are fully cooked before you add the Citrus-Sesame Sauce. Once the initial amount of water has evaporated, check the beans for tenderness, and add another tablespoon or two of water if they are not quite cooked enough. MS

2   teaspoons expeller-pressed canola oil

1   bunch Chinese long beans, about 1 pound, cut into 4- to 6-inch pieces

¼   cup Citrus-Sesame Sauce (page 235)

1   tablespoon toasted sesame seeds

Heat the oil in a skillet over medium-high heat. Add the beans and sauté briefly. Add 1 tablespoon water, cover, and cook for 1 minute, shaking the skillet to move the beans around. Remove the lid and cook the beans until they are tender but still crisp. Add the Citrus-Sesame Sauce and toss to coat. Transfer to a serving plate and sprinkle with the sesame seeds before serving.

Healthy Heating, Healthy Eating

There are endless ways to heat food, from open-fire roasting to microwaving to *sous vide* (a modern French method in which food is gently cooked in vacuum-sealed plastic bags). But both at True Food Kitchen and in my home, I keep it simple, with a short repertoire of basic cooking methods that are neither prehistoric nor high-tech and that don't cause unhealthy changes in food. In general, cooking briefly or at lower temperatures is safer and better. Searing and blackening foods, especially animal protein, is not a good idea.

Among my favorite cooking methods is stir-frying. Stir-frying bite-size pieces of vegetables and protein in good oils (extra-virgin olive or organic expeller-pressed canola or grapeseed) in a wok or nonstick skillet (I prefer the new ceramic-coated ones) is forgiving and fuel efficient, as the precut ingredients can cook in as little as five minutes. I often employ a slight variation I call "steam frying": sautéing food briefly in a little oil, then adding water, stock, or wine and covering the pan. I let the food cook until it's almost done, then uncover and boil off any excess liquid. Liquid in the frying pan keeps the temperature of the food in the safe range.

I often steam vegetables and fish, a particularly healthy technique because it does the least damage to nutrients. As a bonus, it is quick to clean up and very energy efficient. Rather than wrestling with a temperamental, three-legged steamer insert, invest in a true pot-and-steamer combination to avoid spilled contents and burned fingers. Add thick, dense vegetables such as potatoes and corn first, fish such as salmon at the midpoint, and delicate greens last. Generally, when you can smell the food, it's done.

Roasting is another great way to prepare vegetables, especially in winter, when root veggies are abundant and extra heat in the kitchen is a blessing. Any vegetable with some thickness to it, such as carrots, turnips, or asparagus, will take on a complex, mildly sweet flavor as its sugars slowly caramelize in a hot oven. Cut the vegetables into thumb-size pieces, spread on a baking sheet lined with a reusable silicone mat or parchment paper, sprinkle liberally with olive oil, add a few pinches of salt, and bake at 450°F for 15 to 45 minutes, depending on the size, volume, and density of the plants. I've found no better way to win over die-hard veggie-phobes than to introduce them to the joy of well-roasted Brussels sprouts.

To make pizzas at True Food, we use a gas-fired pizza oven. Its ceramic floor and walls radiate heat, creating the crunchy exterior and chewy interior of amazing crust. You can do something similar at home with a pizza stone, available at any well-stocked kitchen supply store. Preheat it thoroughly in the center of your oven. Sprinkle a wooden peel—from the same kitchen store—liberally with cornmeal, and use it to slide the pizza onto the stone.

The movement must be quick and confident—no second thoughts! The results make practicing (and a few pizzas on the floor) worthwhile.

As the weather warms, I enjoy grilling, but it's well known that high-temperature barbecuing (and broiling) of foods that contain fat and protein—especially animal protein—makes carcinogenic compounds. If you do grill meats, use leaner cuts and marinate them before cooking. Marinating reduces the risk, more so if you include spices and herbs like ginger, rosemary, and turmeric. And avoid lighter fluid or self-starting packages of briquettes in a charcoal grill; these will leave residues of toxic chemicals on your food. A healthy alternative is an inexpensive "chimney lighter," which uses a small amount of newspaper to ignite a mass of charcoal in a large metal cylinder. Gas grills are good alternatives to those that use charcoal.

I can't leave the subject of cooking without confronting the argument that heating food in any way is harmful.

Raw foodists argue that cooking destroys vital enzymes. My response: so does stomach acid, and enzymes in plant foods don't play a role in human nutrition. Furthermore, some key nutrients in vegetables are less available when you eat them raw rather than cooked. That's true for carotenoids such as lycopene, which you get from cooked tomatoes, not raw ones, and which protects against prostate cancer. Also, natural toxins in roots, seeds, stems, and leaves are destroyed by cooking. Alfalfa sprouts and other raw legume sprouts contain compounds that can harm the immune system, and raw mushrooms contain natural toxins. Cooking eliminates them, as well as making many foods tastier.

At True Food Kitchen, we serve a mix of raw and cooked foods. And we're proud to have our cooks and kitchens on display. We also offer cooking classes, demonstrating healthy techniques and giving our customers ideas and inspiration to make our kind of food at home. MS

Roasted Glazed Butternut Squash

I love all types of winter squash, but butternut is my favorite. Its name is perfect—the squash has a buttery mouthfeel and sweet, nutty flavor. To get the most out of winter squash, roast them until brown, which means that their plant sugars have caramelized. Since butternut tends to dry out when cooked in the oven, I blanch it before roasting. MS

1	large butternut squash, peeled, seeded, and cut into 2-inch cubes (5 to 6 cups)
⅓	cup Mushroom Stock (page 238)
2	tablespoons balsamic vinegar
1	tablespoon extra-virgin olive oil
¼	teaspoon salt
6	fresh sage leaves, sliced
⅓	cup grated Parmigiano-Reggiano cheese

1. Preheat the oven to 400°F.

2. Place the squash in a large pot and cover with cold water. Bring to a boil and cook until just tender when pierced with a knife, 2 to 3 minutes. Drain well in a colander.

3. Place the squash in a roasting pan. Add the Mushroom Stock, vinegar, oil, salt, and sage and toss well. Sprinkle the cheese on top. Bake the squash, uncovered, for 30 minutes or until golden brown on top. Serve hot.

Stir-Fried Eggplant with Honey, Turmeric, and Soy

Elongated rather than round, Japanese eggplants have thinner skins and cook much more quickly than other varieties, making them ideal for stir-frying. "Sear and stir" is the name of the game when you are using a wok or skillet for this method; the food will burn unless constantly stirred. When using a wok—or a skillet—to stir-fry, heat the pan over the highest heat possible. (Make sure you turn on the exhaust ventilation, too.) Eggplant is spongy and sucks up a lot of liquid while cooking. Don't add more oil to the pan; just continue to sear and stir until the eggplant is well cooked. MS

2	tablespoons low-sodium soy sauce
1	tablespoon honey
½	teaspoon red pepper flakes
¼	teaspoon ground turmeric
1	tablespoon expeller-pressed canola oil
4	cups Japanese eggplant, sliced on the bias into ½-inch pieces (about 2 eggplants)
1½	cups thinly sliced onions
1	scallion, thinly sliced

1. In a bowl, whisk together the soy sauce, honey, red pepper flakes, turmeric, and 2 tablespoons water.

2. Heat a wok or skillet over high heat. Add the oil. When hot, add the eggplant and onions. Let the vegetables sear for a moment, then stir-fry by tossing them with a wooden spatula for 3 to 5 minutes. Add one-half of the turmeric-soy mixture, then more if the eggplant is too dry. Transfer to a serving dish, sprinkle with the scallion, and serve.

Stir-Fried Brussels Sprouts with Umami Sauce

MAKES 4 TO 6 SERVINGS

Most people who say they hate Brussels sprouts have never had them properly prepared. The secrets: Choose fresh, smallish, young sprouts; do not overcook them; and enhance them with the right seasonings. Here, halved sprouts are quickly stir-fried with garlic, then tossed in True Food's Umami Sauce. Spring these on a Brussels sprouts hater and change a life. MS

1½ teaspoons expeller-pressed canola oil

1½ pounds Brussels sprouts, halved

2 garlic cloves, thinly sliced

⅓ cup Umami Sauce (page 236)

2 teaspoons freshly squeezed lemon juice

½ teaspoon freshly grated lemon zest

¼ teaspoon salt

¼ teaspoon freshly ground black pepper

Heat a wok or skillet over high heat. Add the oil. When hot, add the Brussels sprouts and garlic, and sauté for 1 minute. Add ¼ cup water, cover, and cook for 2 minutes, tossing to cook evenly. Remove the cover and stir in the Umami Sauce, lemon juice, zest, salt, and pepper. Continue to cook while occasionally tossing until the liquid is reduced to a thick sauce, about 7 minutes. Transfer to a plate and serve hot.

Grilled Artichokes

This is my favorite way to prepare artichokes, and the bigger, the better. Boiling whole artichokes makes them soggy; steaming is better but leaves them flavorless and in need of a fatty dip. My preferred method—steaming, then grilling the vegetables until crisp—makes eating the leaves and heart very pleasurable. If the artichokes are quite large, half of one will be a good serving. AW

4   large artichokes

¼   cup extra-virgin olive oil

¼   cup balsamic vinegar

1   teaspoon salt

½   teaspoon freshly ground black pepper

1. Put 2 inches water into a pot large enough to hold the artichokes in a steaming basket. Insert the steaming basket.

2. Place the artichokes in the steaming basket, cover the pot, and bring the water to a boil. Steam the artichokes until just tender, 30 to 40 minutes. The artichokes are cooked when a leaf can be easily pulled off or the base can be easily pierced with a knife. Using tongs, transfer the artichokes to a plate and cool.

3. Using a serrated knife, cut the artichokes in half lengthwise. With a spoon, remove the fuzzy chokes and any purple-tinged leaves.

4. Divide the olive oil, balsamic vinegar, salt and pepper, and ¼ cup water between 2 gallon-size resealable plastic freezer bags. Seal and shake well. Place the cooked artichokes in the plastic bags, seal, and shake to coat all sides. Marinate overnight in the refrigerator or for at least 1 hour.

5. Preheat the grill to medium. Place the artichokes cut side down on the grill. Grill until lightly browned, 5 to 7 minutes. Turn the artichokes over and grill until the tips are lightly charred, 3 to 4 minutes. Serve hot or at room temperature.

Grilled Sweet Potatoes, Yakitori-Style

Yakitori means "grilled fowl" in Japanese, but the term has come to refer to any food cooked on a skewer. The sweet potatoes tend to stick to the grill if it is not clean and hot, so make sure the grate is well scrubbed, fully heated, and liberally oiled (in that order) to boost your odds of success. My kids love these; they make a good side dish for grilled chicken or turkey burgers. If using bamboo skewers, soak them in water for 20 minutes to keep them from burning. MS

5	sweet potatoes, sliced into ¾-inch-thick rounds
¼	cup sake
¼	cup mirin
¼	cup low-sodium soy sauce
2	tablespoons honey
1	tablespoon evaporated cane sugar
1½	teaspoons grated fresh ginger
1	tablespoon dark sesame oil
1	tablespoon toasted sesame seeds

1. Preheat the grill to high. Using a paper towel, rub the grill with expeller-pressed canola oil.

2. Insert a steamer basket into a pot filled with 1 to 2 inches water. Line the basket with the sliced sweet potatoes, cover, turn on the heat, and steam until tender but still a bit firm, 8 to 10 minutes. Let cool. While the sweet potatoes are cooking, combine the sake, mirin, soy sauce, honey, sugar, and ginger in a small saucepan. Bring to a boil, and then reduce the heat to a low simmer. Simmer for 10 minutes, and then remove the glaze from the heat.

3. Thread the sweet potatoes onto skewers. Brush the skewered sweet potatoes with the sesame oil and place on the hot grill. Baste the sweet potatoes on both sides with the glaze. Baste repeatedly with the glaze and cook on both sides until the sweet potatoes are lightly charred. Transfer the skewers to a serving platter, garnish with the sesame seeds, and serve.

Smoked Peppers with Red Onion Relish

MAKES 4 TO 6 SERVINGS

I learned to make this combination of smoked peppers, red onions, and honey from Alex Stratta, one of my mentors. I like to serve this with spring lamb or falafel, or as an appetizer atop arugula with some black olives. MS

3	red bell peppers
2	yellow bell peppers
½	cup mesquite chips
2	teaspoons extra-virgin olive oil
1	small red onion, sliced
3	garlic cloves, sliced
1½	teaspoons chopped fresh oregano
1	tablespoon honey
1	tablespoon apple cider vinegar
¼	teaspoon salt
¼	teaspoon freshly ground black pepper

1. Preheat the grill to medium heat.

2. Roast the bell peppers over a gas flame or in a broiler until they char, turning them occasionally to blacken all sides. Place in a bowl and cover with plastic wrap. Let cool so that the skins loosen. While they are cooling, place the mesquite chips in a bowl with 1 cup water to soak.

3. When the peppers are cool enough to handle, peel and seed them. Slice them into ¼-inch strips. Place the peppers in a disposable aluminum pan. Drain the water from the mesquite chips. If you have a charcoal or wood-burning grill, place the damp mesquite chips directly on the coals. If you have a gas grill, place the wood chips in another foil pan and place it on the flames. Cover the grill. Once you see smoke, uncover the grill and place the pan with the peppers on the grill. Cover and let the peppers smoke for about 10 minutes.

4. Heat the oil in a skillet over medium heat. Add the onion and sauté for 2 to 3 minutes, until it begins to soften. Add the garlic and sauté for 1 minute. Stir in the smoked peppers, oregano, honey, vinegar, salt, and pepper. Raise the heat to medium-high and cook until there is very little liquid in the pan, 2 to 3 minutes. Adjust the seasonings and serve hot or at room temperature.

Braised Broccoli with Orange and Parmesan

MAKES 4 TO 6 SERVINGS

My children like broccoli, and because it is so healthy I am happy to give it to them on a regular basis. With my kids, simpler is usually better, but in this case, the sweet-and-sour effect of the orange and tomato juices combined with a sprinkle of fresh Parmesan makes them really love this dish. No vegetable suffers more from overcooking than broccoli, so watch it carefully! MS

¼ cup freshly squeezed orange juice

1 (14-ounce) can crushed San Marzano tomatoes

1 head broccoli, cut into florets, stalks peeled and sliced

¼ teaspoon chopped fresh oregano

¼ teaspoon red pepper flakes

¼ teaspoon salt

⅛ teaspoon freshly ground black pepper

1 tablespoon extra-virgin olive oil

¼ cup Parmigiano-Reggiano cheese shavings

Combine the orange juice and tomatoes in a medium pot over medium-high heat. Bring to a boil and then add the broccoli. Add the oregano and pepper flakes. Cover and cook until tender yet still crisp and bright green, about 3 minutes. Remove the lid and season with the salt and pepper. Transfer to a serving dish. Drizzle with the olive oil, sprinkle on the Parmesan shavings, and serve.

French Bean Salad with Vegetarian Caesar Dressing

MAKES 4 TO 6 SERVINGS

Here's a variation of a dish my mother used to make when I was growing up in Oregon, with a vegetarian Caesar dressing created by Andy's daughter, Diana. Talk about a collaboration! As always, freshness and seasonality are the keys to the success of this dish. It's best when made a few hours in advance and served chilled. Diana first used this dressing on vegetarian Caesar salad. Try it tossed with romaine leaves, croutons, and some Parmigiano-Reggiano shavings. MS

1   pound fingerling potatoes, cubed

1   tablespoon plus 1½ teaspoons extra-virgin olive oil

¼   teaspoon salt

¼   teaspoon freshly ground black pepper

10 ounces green beans, stemmed and strings removed

2   medium zucchini, cut into thin half-moons

⅓   cup chopped Marcona almonds

¾   cup sliced Oven-Roasted Tomatoes (page 240)

1   cup canned kidney beans, rinsed and drained

⅓   cup pitted and sliced Kalamata olives

3   tablespoons chopped fresh basil

⅓   cup Vegetarian Caesar Dressing (page 233)

1. Preheat the oven to 400°F. Line a baking sheet with aluminum foil.

2. Arrange the potato cubes on the prepared baking sheet and toss them with the olive oil, salt, and pepper. Roast for 25 minutes, or until tender when pierced with a knife. Remove from the oven and set aside.

3. Bring a saucepan of salted water to a boil. Add the green beans and cook for 4 to 5 minutes. Drain and rinse under cold water.

4. In a large bowl, combine the potatoes, green beans, and all of the remaining ingredients, tossing to coat evenly with the Vegetarian Caesar Dressing. Adjust the seasonings with more salt and pepper if necessary. Let marinate for 15 minutes before serving.

Following the Farmer

When I first started to cook, I began with recipes, then went shopping for the ingredients I needed. Shopping meant going to a local supermarket. I first experienced real markets during the years I lived in South America and later when I traveled in Asia. These were usually in the town and city centers, where farmers and vendors of all kinds came once or twice a week to sell their goods.

I find the best way to get to know a place in many parts of the world is to arrive on market day, brave the crowds, and wander the stalls. I always head first for the produce section to see what local farms are producing, and when I come across particularly appealing vegetables and herbs, I think about how I might best use them. I let the ingredients dictate recipes and meal planning, not the reverse. I now do the same at home, taking advantage of whatever is at peak flavor and most abundant in my garden. As soon as the black kale is ready, I start using it raw in salads; if I can't keep up with it, I make batches of Kale Pesto (page 234). If I have ripe tomatoes, of course I feature them in my dishes.

I also see what is available and best at local farmers' markets and plan meals accordingly. For a recent Thanksgiving dinner, I wanted to grill a whole fish but had no other dishes in mind. I left the selection of fish to my favorite fishmonger and was delighted with the organically raised Scottish salmon he delivered. A friend sent me dried black trumpet mushrooms he had picked in northern California; I reconstituted them in broth, sautéed them in olive oil, and added them to wild rice. Beautiful Brussels sprouts and artichokes were in season. I roasted the former and grilled the latter (see page 181). And I turned a great-looking organic kabocha pumpkin I found

at a farmers' market into a vegan squash pie.

Michael Stebner has long cooked this way, following the farmers in southern California when he had his own restaurant there and doing the same when he moved to Arizona. Like me, he finds that at any time of year a few kinds of fruits and vegetables are always best to use. It's never entirely predictable. Japanese cucumbers might be a good bet in late June, but dozens of variables in weather, soil, pests, and freshness can make them a terrible choice. Extra-early Cherokee Purple heirloom tomatoes may happen, this year only, to be amazing.

In order to take advantage of the best of local farms for True Food Kitchen, Michael developed relationships— that quickly became friendships—with farmers. "I always need to know what's happening at the farms," he says. "For some chefs, sourcing is the smallest part of the job. For me, it's the most important."

Michael has introduced me to a number of his farmer friends, and together we have toured farmers' markets in California and Arizona, always looking for What's Best Today. If he finds something wonderful, he might ask me for suggestions for using it. Recently, when he told me about an abundant supply of plump, green Arizona pistachios, I asked him to put Pistachio Dream (page 213) on the menu. And he's surprised me with ever-changing seasonal salads, always using the freshest, most colorful, most flavorful local vegetables.

I'm delighted by the appearance of more and more farmers' markets in our country. If you get in the habit of shopping at them, you can begin to plan your meals around what's best and most available from the land in your area. When you go, leave your shopping list behind.

Another way for home cooks to follow the farmer is to join a Community Supported Agriculture (CSA) organization. (The website localharvest.org/csa has a comprehensive, nationwide list.) In return for a monthly subscription fee, you get boxes of produce directly from a farm, the contents determined by the farmer. For Americans used to choosing from predictable (and uniformly mediocre) produce in supermarkets, the surprise element requires adjustment. If you open your CSA box with dread, hoping it has this and not that, you have some distance to go. If you attack it with roughly the same enthusiasm as a child opening presents on Christmas and are delighted by whatever you find, you are on the right track.

Ultimately, getting your produce should become a kind of meditative practice. Abandon preconceived notions and desires and accept whatever the moment—and the market—brings. It will lead you to discovery, growth, and memorable meals. AW

Summer Vegetable Casserole

MAKES 4 TO 6 SERVINGS

This is my version of a Provençal dish served in high-end restaurants—including several in which I have worked—called confit byaldi. *It is substantial enough to be the main course but so simple it could also be a side dish. The Parmesan bread crumbs are terrific sprinkled on pasta or salad, so make extra. You can prepare the Eggplant Relish and Braised Fennel ahead of time and then put the whole thing together the next day.* MS

EGGPLANT RELISH
Makes about 2 cups

3   tablespoons extra-virgin
     olive oil

1   medium onion, diced

1   small eggplant, cubed
     (about 2 cups)

¼   teaspoon salt

⅓   cup Oven-Roasted
     Tomatoes (page 240)

4   garlic cloves, minced

2   teaspoons balsamic
     vinegar

1½   teaspoons chopped
     fresh sage

1½   teaspoons chopped
     fresh rosemary

     Pinch of cayenne pepper

1. Heat the oil in a large skillet over medium-high heat until it shimmers. Add the onion and eggplant, season with the salt, and cook until the eggplant begins to brown and the onions are translucent. Add the tomatoes and garlic and continue to cook for 2 minutes. Remove from the heat and let cool for 10 to 15 minutes. Transfer to a blender or food processor. Add the vinegar, sage, rosemary, and cayenne and pulse until chunky, not pureed. Transfer to a bowl and set aside.

BRAISED FENNEL

1   tablespoon extra-virgin
     olive oil

2   tablespoons diced onion

1   medium fennel bulb, diced

1   teaspoon freshly grated
     orange zest

2   tablespoons freshly
     squeezed orange juice

¼   cup dry white wine

¼   teaspoon salt

⅛   teaspoon freshly ground
     black pepper

2. Heat the oil in a large skillet over medium-high heat until it shimmers. Add the onion and fennel and sauté until just tender. Add the zest, juice, wine, salt, and pepper and cook until no liquid remains, about 5 minutes. Remove from the heat and set aside.

Continues »

PARMESAN-BREAD CRUMB TOPPING

3/4 cup freshly grated
     Parmigiano-Reggiano cheese

1/2 cup whole wheat bread crumbs

1   garlic clove, mashed

2   teaspoons chopped
     fresh oregano

2   teaspoons chopped
     fresh thyme

3. Combine all of the Parmesan-Bread Crumb Topping ingredients in a bowl and set aside.

CASSEROLE

1   red bell pepper

1   small eggplant, thinly sliced

1   medium zucchini, thinly sliced

1   medium yellow squash,
     thinly sliced

1/2 teaspoon salt

2   tablespoons extra-virgin
     olive oil

4. Roast the red pepper over a gas flame or in a broiler until it chars, turning it occasionally to blacken all sides. Place in a bowl and cover with plastic wrap. When the pepper is cool enough to handle, peel and seed it. Slice it into 1/4-inch strips.

5. Preheat the oven to 350°F.

6. Arrange the eggplant, zucchini, and squash in a single layer on a work surface covered with a clean kitchen towel. Sprinkle evenly with the salt and let sit for 10 minutes. Using paper towels or another clean kitchen towel, pat away the moisture on the vegetables' surfaces.

7. Heat the oil in a large skillet over medium-high heat until it shimmers. Sauté the eggplant slices until they are tender, and then transfer to a plate.

8. Lightly oil a 3-quart shallow ceramic baking pan. Arrange half of the eggplant slices on the bottom of the pan. Top with half of the Braised Fennel, then spread on half of the Eggplant Relish. Fan half of the zucchini, squash, and roasted red pepper slices over the relish. Repeat the layering with the eggplant slices, Braised Fennel, and Eggplant Relish. Add a layer of roasted red pepper and then top with the remaining zucchini and squash.

9. Cover with foil and bake until heated through but not bubbling, 30 to 40 minutes. Remove the pan and turn the oven to broil. Sprinkle on the Parmesan-Bread Crumb Topping and broil until golden brown, 5 to 7 minutes. Remove and let sit for 5 minutes before serving.

Sweet Potato Gratin, Indian-Style

Traditional French gratins are made with lots of cream, cheese, and butter. Asian staples—coconut cream, turmeric, and curry—supply bold flavors and richness in this sweet potato gratin. MS

1 (15-ounce) can coconut cream

2 tablespoons packed dark brown sugar

1 teaspoon ground turmeric

2 teaspoons garam masala

¼ teaspoon cayenne pepper

¼ teaspoon salt

¼ teaspoon freshly ground black pepper

4 sweet potatoes, peeled and thinly sliced

½ cup Cashew Milk (page 239)

1. Put one oven rack in the upper part of the oven and another one in the lower part. Preheat the oven to 350°F. Line a baking sheet with aluminum foil.

2. In a large bowl, whisk together the coconut cream, sugar, turmeric, garam masala, cayenne, salt, and pepper. Add the potatoes and toss to coat. Arrange the potatoes in a shallow 2- to 3-quart baking dish. Pour any remaining liquid over the potatoes. Cover with aluminum foil.

3. Put the foil-lined baking sheet on the lower rack to catch any juices. Bake the gratin on the upper rack for 45 to 50 minutes, or until tender when pierced with a skewer or fork. Remove the foil and bake for another 5 to 10 minutes to lightly brown the top layer. Remove from the oven and let sit for 5 minutes. Garnish each serving with a spoonful of the Cashew Milk.

Spaghetti Squash and Zucchini Parmesan

MAKES 4 TO 6 SERVINGS

When cooked, spaghetti squash separates into strings that can be sauced or otherwise used like pasta, making it a delightful gluten-free, low-carbohydrate alternative. When roasting the squash, make sure the skins are nicely browned; this will impart a deeper flavor to the flesh. Make enough for leftovers; it is even tastier the second day. MS

1   large spaghetti squash (2 to 3 pounds)

1   large zucchini, grated

⅓ cup Caramelized Onions (page 240)

1   cup Tomato Sauce (page 236)

Salt and freshly ground black pepper

6   ounces mozzarella cheese, grated

½ cup freshly grated Parmigiano-Reggiano cheese

1. Preheat the oven to 350°F.

2. Pierce the spaghetti squash with a fork in several places. Microwave it on high power for 12 minutes, rotating it every 3 minutes. Let the squash cool, then cut it in half lengthwise and scoop out the seeds with a spoon. Scoop out the flesh into a large bowl. Add the zucchini, onions, and tomato sauce. Season with salt and pepper. Spoon the mixture into a 3-quart shallow baking pan. Bake for 40 to 45 minutes.

3. Remove the baking pan from the oven and turn the oven to broil. Top the vegetables with the grated cheeses and place under the broiler until golden brown, about 5 minutes. Let sit for 5 to 10 minutes before serving.

Curried Peapods and Tofu

Sugar snap peas are one of my favorite spring vegetables. I grow them in my garden and am always amazed at the prolificacy of the vines. They are best lightly cooked—steamed or stir-fried—until bright green and crunchy-tender. This quick and easy vegan main pairs snap peas with sautéed, pressed tofu in a highly flavored sauce. It's filled with vegetable protein and protective phytonutrients. Make it milder or zestier with snap peas or snow peas or a mixture of both, as you like. AW

2   tablespoons expeller-pressed canola oil

8   ounces firm or pressed tofu, thinly sliced and briefly pressed between paper towels to dry

1   medium onion, sliced

1 to 2 tablespoons curry powder

1   teaspoon evaporated cane sugar

¼   teaspoon salt

½   cup vegetable broth

1   pound sugar snap or snow peas, stemmed and strings removed

¼   cup chopped fresh cilantro

1. Heat 1 tablespoon of the oil in a nonstick skillet over medium-high heat. Add the tofu and sauté until the slices are golden on both sides. Transfer the tofu to a plate.

2. Heat the remaining 1 tablespoon oil in the skillet over medium heat. Add the onion and sauté until translucent. Stir in the curry powder, sugar, and salt and stir-fry for 1 minute. Add the broth and tofu, and stir until combined, taking care not to break up the tofu. Add the peas, cover, and let the peas steam until just crunchy-tender, 2 to 3 minutes. Transfer to a serving dish and garnish with the cilantro before serving.

Braised Red Cabbage

This easy-to-prepare, hearty, and festive dish makes a great addition to winter holiday dinners. In addition to a rich, satisfying flavor, it provides a variety of health-protective phytonutrients. If you add chestnuts (roasted and vacuum-packed chestnuts without preservatives are available) and serve it over noodles, it becomes a main course that goes well with a green salad. AW

2 tablespoons extra-virgin olive oil

1 large onion, sliced

2 carrots, sliced

1 medium head red cabbage, cored and shredded

1 Granny Smith apple, peeled, cored, and diced

1½ cups dry red wine

¼ cup red wine vinegar

3 garlic cloves, minced

2 tablespoons packed light brown sugar

1 teaspoon salt

¼ teaspoon freshly ground black pepper

1 Turkish bay leaf (or ⅓ of a California bay leaf)

½ teaspoon ground cloves

1 (14-ounce) jar roasted chestnuts (optional)

In a large pot, heat the oil over medium-high heat until it shimmers. Add the onion and carrots and sauté until the onion is translucent. Add the cabbage and apple and toss well to coat. Stir in the wine, vinegar, garlic, sugar, salt, pepper, bay leaf, and cloves. Lower the heat to a simmer and cook for 45 minutes, stirring occasionally, until the cabbage is tender. If using the roasted chestnuts, add them after 20 minutes. Remove the bay leaf and adjust the seasoning before serving.

DESSERTS

I do not recommend sweet desserts at the end
of every meal, but the desserts at True Food
Kitchen are spectacular. Many are based on fruit,
none are excessively sweet, and all are served in
moderate portions. And remember that dark
chocolate has a place of honor at the very top of
the Anti-Inflammatory Food Pyramid. AW

Cortes Mixed Berry Crisp

MAKES 8 TO 10 SERVINGS

My summer home on Cortes Island, British Columbia, is berry heaven, with a succession of varieties—strawberries, raspberries, black raspberries, tayberries, blueberries, and finally blackberries at the end of the season. A mixture of berries or all of one kind works well in this crisp covered with an almond-flavored topping. In the autumn, use a combination of sliced apples and fresh cranberries. Almond paste is available in the supermarket baking section, arrowroot powder in the spice section. For a vegan version, substitute Spectrum Spread for the butter. AW

½ cup evaporated cane sugar

2 tablespoons arrowroot powder

8 cups mixed berries

½ cup (8 tablespoons) unsalted butter

½ cup almond paste

1 cup packed light brown sugar

½ teaspoon salt

½ cup all-purpose flour

½ cup whole wheat pastry flour

1 cup old-fashioned rolled oats

Vanilla ice cream or frozen yogurt, for serving (optional)

1. Preheat the oven to 350°F.

2. Whisk together the sugar and arrowroot in a large bowl. Add the berries and toss thoroughly to coat. Divide the fruit mixture among eight 6- to 8-ounce ramekins or spread in a 2-quart shallow baking dish.

3. To make the topping, put the butter, almond paste, brown sugar, and salt in a food processor. Pulse to combine. Add the flours and pulse 2 or 3 times to combine. Transfer the topping mixture to a bowl and fold in the oats. Cover the fruit with the topping.

4. Bake for 30 to 40 minutes, or until the fruit bubbles through the lightly browned topping. Serve warm, with vanilla ice cream or frozen yogurt, if desired.

Chocolate Icebox Tart

Coconut oil was once reviled because it is a saturated fat, but recent research suggests that virgin, non-hydrogenated coconut oil is actually quite heart-healthy. The unique fatty acids in coconut oil do not adversely affect cholesterol ratios in the blood. Serve small pieces of this exceptionally rich, no-bake tart. MS

1 cup unsweetened shredded coconut

¾ cup ground almonds

1⅓ cups unsweetened natural cocoa powder

½ cup agave nectar

1⅓ cups coconut oil

½ cup almond butter

1. In a bowl, mix together the coconut, almonds, ⅓ cup of the cocoa powder, ¼ cup of the agave nectar, and ⅓ cup of the coconut oil. Mix well to make the crust. Press the crust into the bottom and partially up the sides of an 11 by 7 by 2-inch sheet pan or baking dish. Chill for 30 minutes.

2. Put the almond butter and the remaining 1 cup cocoa powder, ¼ cup agave nectar, and 1 cup coconut oil in a food processor. Blend until smooth, stopping to scrape down the sides of the bowl. Pour the filling into the chilled tart shell and chill for 2 hours or until firm. Cut into 1-inch squares and serve. Cover and refrigerate any left over for up to 3 days.

Chocolate-Banana Tart

MAKES SIX 3-INCH TARTS; 6 SERVINGS

Finding interesting regional products like mesquite flour and integrating them into novel dishes such as this banana tart is one of the most rewarding parts of my work. Mesquite flour is made from the flat, dried pods of the mesquite tree—the whole pods are ground to create a dark, rich flour that is subtly sweet, with fruity overtones. Mesquite flour is combined here with spelt flour to make round pastry disks, which are frosted with chocolate ganache, then topped with bananas, Brazil nuts, and a dollop of whipped cream. If you don't have mesquite and spelt flours, substitute whole wheat pastry flour for the mesquite and whole wheat flour for the spelt. MS

¾ cup spelt flour

⅓ cup mesquite flour

½ cup old-fashioned rolled oats

¼ teaspoon baking soda

¼ teaspoon baking powder

¼ teaspoon salt

⅓ cup (5 ⅓ tablespoons) unsalted butter, cubed and softened

½ cup plus 2 tablespoons evaporated cane sugar

1½ teaspoons agave nectar

3 large eggs

¼ teaspoon vanilla extract

3 tablespoons finely chopped plus ¼ cup chopped raw Brazil nuts

¾ cup heavy cream

2 ounces 70% organic dark chocolate, broken up into small pieces

3 bananas, thinly sliced

1. Preheat the oven to 300°F. Line two baking sheets with silicone baking mats or parchment paper.

2. Stir the flours, oats, baking soda, baking powder, and salt together in a bowl.

3. In a standing mixer, combine the butter and ½ cup of the sugar. Cream the mixture until light in color and smooth, about 4 minutes. Add the agave and blend. Add the eggs one at a time, blending between each addition. Add the vanilla. On low speed, add the flour mixture and mix until the batter is the consistency of cookie dough.

4. Using a spatula, fold in the 3 tablespoons finely chopped nuts by hand. Turn the dough out onto a lightly floured work surface and flatten into a disk. Wrap in plastic wrap and refrigerate for 2 hours.

5. Turn the dough out onto a lightly floured work surface. Using a rolling pin, roll out the dough to a ¼-inch thickness. Using a 3-inch round cookie cutter, cut out 6 pastry bases. Using a large spatula, place the dough on the prepared baking sheets and bake until golden brown, about 8 minutes. Transfer the pastry rounds to a wire rack to cool.

6. To make the ganache, bring ¼ cup of the cream to a boil in a saucepan. Remove from the heat. Add the chocolate to the cream and let sit for 3 to 5 minutes so the chocolate melts. Whisk together until smooth. Set aside.

7. Preheat the oven to broil.

8. To assemble the tarts, place the pastry rounds back on the baking sheets and divide the ganache among the pastry rounds, using an offset spatula or dinner knife to spread the ganache to the edges. Arrange the banana slices on top of the ganache in a pinwheel pattern. Sprinkle the remaining 2 tablespoons sugar over the bananas and put the tarts under the broiler for 30 seconds to brown the tops. Watch them carefully so they don't burn.

9. Whip the remaining $1/2$ cup cream to soft peaks, and add a spoonful to each tart. Garnish with the $1/4$ cup chopped nuts before serving.

Sweets and Sweeteners

One of the most disturbing areas of nutrition research is the growing body of scientific evidence on the harmful effects of sugar. Everybody knows that too much sugar in the diet is often associated with obesity, poor dental health, and possibly mood and energy swings, but the new findings have to do with serious disturbance of liver function and long-term health.

The problem is fructose, sometimes referred to as "fruit sugar," which is present in all common sweeteners. Table sugar (sucrose) is 50 percent fructose—a bigger percentage than in some varieties of high-fructose corn syrup. There's a lot of fructose in honey, agave nectar, and maple syrup. And our bodies can't digest it.

In the distant past, people got fructose only from ripe fruit (which contains much less of it than fruit juice or today's sweeteners) and an occasional honeycomb (guarded by bees). The small amount they ate did not damage their livers. Today, most people are consuming fructose in large amounts every day, especially in sweetened beverages, fruit juices, and desserts. As a result, doctors are seeing an epidemic of a once rare problem: nonalcoholic fatty liver disease, which itself often produces no symptoms but is strongly associated with obesity, insulin resistance, hypertension, type 2 diabetes, and cardiovascular disease. It is marked by accumulation of fat in liver cells, the human version of foie gras. Excess fructose in the diet is the main cause.

That means we should cut down on sweets—all sweets. High-fructose corn syrup is a cheap sweetener and a marker of low-quality food products, but really, it's no worse for our health than table sugar or honey. The fiber present in whole fruit blunts the effect of its sugar content, but the new view of fructose means that a glass of apple juice (whether fresh squeezed, frozen, or bottled) is not much different from a soft drink.

What are we to do with this information? We are born with a sweet tooth, probably because in the distant past when sugar was scarce, individuals who managed to find and consume it got bursts of energy that helped them survive. Evolution did not prepare us for the abundance and ready availability of sugar that we have today. My advice is to avoid drinks and snacks that contain added, refined sweeteners, to cut down on the use of all sweeteners, and to have desserts occasionally rather than with every meal.

At True Food Kitchen, we make our desserts less sweet than people might expect, incorporate fruit into many, use a variety of natural sweeteners, and make them roughly one-third the portion size of typical restaurant desserts. I enjoy them very much as occasional treats and suggest you use them that way, too.

If I crave something sweet after a meal or for a snack, I usually go for a piece of high-quality, plain dark chocolate with at least 70 percent cocoa. The amount of sugar in it is small, and if I let it slowly melt in my mouth, it gives me much pleasure. AW

Chocolate Pudding

MAKES 4 TO 6 SERVINGS

This version of a classic favorite is dairy-free, gluten-free, and vegan. Cocoa powder and dark chocolate intensify the pudding's flavor; this is a good way to enjoy the health benefits of chocolate. MS

1½ cups evaporated cane sugar

1   cup unsweetened natural cocoa powder

1   tablespoon plus 2¼ teaspoons cornstarch

3½ cups plain soy milk

9   ounces 70% organic dark chocolate, coarsely chopped

1   teaspoon vanilla extract

     Vanilla bean seeds scraped from 1 halved vanilla bean

½   teaspoon ground cinnamon

⅓   cup coarsely chopped raw unsalted pistachios

⅓   cup coarsely chopped walnuts

1. Fill a large bowl with ice and water. Set aside.

2. Combine the sugar, cocoa powder, and cornstarch in a saucepan. Whisk in half of the soy milk to create a smooth paste. Add the remaining soy milk and whisk to combine. Place over medium-high heat. Stirring constantly, bring the mixture to a simmer. Remove from the heat and whisk in the chocolate, vanilla extract, vanilla bean seeds, and cinnamon.

3. Strain the pudding mixture through a fine-mesh sieve into a bowl. Immediately set the bowl in the ice bath to cool down the pudding. Place a piece of plastic wrap directly on the pudding's surface to prevent a skin from forming. Refrigerate for at least 4 hours before serving.

4. Divide the pudding among four to six 6-ounce bowls or ramekins. Top with the pistachios and walnuts and serve.

Coconut–Black Rice Pudding

I've enjoyed this Asian comfort food at street stalls in Thailand and often serve it at holiday dinners, using all-American maple syrup to sweeten my version. Black sweet rice, which turns deep purple when cooked, is often labeled as "forbidden rice," because legend has it that only Chinese emperors were allowed to eat it. It is available at natural foods stores and online from Gold Mine Natural Foods (goldminenaturalfoods.com). Plan ahead before making this, as the rice needs to soak in water for at least 4 hours before you cook it. AW

1³⁄4 cups black sweet rice

1   (14-ounce) can light coconut milk

¹⁄2 cup maple syrup

¹⁄2 generous cup unsweetened shredded coconut

¹⁄2 teaspoon salt

2 to 3 bananas, sliced

     Coconut sorbet or vanilla ice cream, for serving (optional)

1. Put the rice in a strainer and rinse with running water. Drain the rice and put it into a pot with 3 cups cold water. Let stand at room temperature for at least 4 hours or overnight.

2. Remove, but do not discard, 1¹⁄2 cups of the water, leaving the rest in the pot for cooking the rice.

3. Stir in the coconut milk, maple syrup, coconut, and salt. Bring the mixture to a boil, then cover, reduce the heat to low, and simmer, stirring occasionally, until the rice is soupy, about 1 hour.

4. Stir in the bananas and continue cooking until most of the liquid is absorbed. Taste the rice for doneness. If it is chewier than you like, add ¹⁄2 cup of the reserved soaking water at a time and continue cooking. The rice should be tender but chewy.

5. Remove the pudding from the heat and let stand, covered, for 15 minutes. Serve warm with a scoop of coconut sorbet or vanilla ice cream, if you like.

Pistachio Dream

Most nondairy frozen desserts are disappointing—or worse. I don't like the bean-y undertone of soy milk or the strange flavor of rice milk in them. Nut milks are perfect. This traditional Middle Eastern classic uses easy-to-make pistachio milk. Bottled rose water—a little goes a long way—can be found in many supermarkets or Middle Eastern markets. AW

2   cups raw unsalted pistachios

½   cup evaporated cane sugar

¼   teaspoon salt

1   teaspoon almond extract

½   teaspoon rose water

1. Chill the ice cream machine canister in the freezer according to the manufacturer's directions.

2. Grind the pistachios to a fine powder in a blender, stopping and stirring with a chopstick occasionally. Add 4 cups water and blend on high for 2 minutes. Add the sugar and salt and blend.

3. Strain the pistachio mixture through a fine-mesh sieve over a bowl, pressing down on the solids to get out all the milk. Stir in the almond extract and rose water. Chill the mixture for 2 to 4 hours; it must be cold before going into the ice cream machine.

4. Pour the mixture into the machine's frozen canister and freeze according to the manufacturer's directions.

Lemon-Ginger Frozen Yogurt

This my homemade answer to the frozen yogurt craze. Organic Greek-style yogurt imparts a subtle acidity. Ginger, with its antioxidant and anti-inflammatory health benefits, gives this refreshing frozen treat some zing. Serve atop seasonal berries in summer or garnish with pomegranate seeds in winter. Homemade frozen yogurt, which lacks stabilizers and emulsifiers, doesn't keep well in the freezer like commercial brands, so serve it the same day you make it. MS

3/4 cup evaporated cane sugar

1/4 cup Simple Syrup (see page 242)

1/2 cup grated fresh ginger

2 cups organic full-fat Greek-style plain yogurt

Zest of 1 lemon

Juice of 1 lemon

1. Chill the ice cream machine canister in the freezer according to the manufacturer's directions.

2. Combine 3/4 cup water, the sugar, Simple Syrup, and ginger in a saucepan and bring to a boil. Turn off the heat and let steep for 10 minutes.

3. Combine the yogurt, lemon zest, and lemon juice in a bowl. Strain the ginger syrup through a fine-mesh sieve into the yogurt-citrus mixture and whisk until smooth. Chill the mixture for 2 to 4 hours; it must be cold before going into the ice cream machine.

4. Pour the mixture into the machine's canister and freeze according to the manufacturer's directions.

Orange and Sea Buckthorn Sorbet

MAKES 1 QUART; 4 TO 6 SERVINGS

Shortly after we met, Andy introduced me to sea buckthorn juice and asked if I could do anything with it. The flavor is definitely assertive—sharply sour and pungent, like dried apricots. At first I thought it would overwhelm almost anything, but with a little experimentation, I found that sea buckthorn enhances the flavor of citrus fruits. The vanilla bean adds richness and smoothes out the acidity. MS

3   cups freshly squeezed orange juice

⅓   cup sea buckthorn juice

¼   cup agave nectar

   Vanilla bean seeds scraped from 2 halved vanilla beans

1. Chill the ice cream machine canister in the freezer according to the manufacturer's directions.

2. Whisk together all of the ingredients in a bowl. Chill the mixture for 2 to 4 hours; it must be cold before going into the ice cream machine.

3. Pour the mixture into the machine's frozen canister and freeze according to the manufacturer's directions.

Pomegranate-Yuzu Sorbet

MAKES 1 QUART; 4 TO 6 SERVINGS

Yuzu is a citrus fruit native to eastern Asia. It is tart, similar to grapefruit but with mandarin orange notes. The zest is the most prized part of the fruit, but in this part of the world the juice is often the only product available at the market. In Phoenix, our local organic farm, McClendon's Select, has fresh yuzu available for a short period each winter. Asian and other markets sell bottled yuzu juice. Buy the best brand you can find; cheap ones often have a soapy flavor. MS

1   **cup evaporated cane sugar**

2   **cups unsweetened pomegranate juice**

1   **cup freshly squeezed orange juice**

1/3 **cup yuzu juice**

1. Chill the ice cream machine canister in the freezer according to the manufacturer's directions.

2. Combine the sugar and $2/3$ cup hot water in a bowl; whisk until the sugar is dissolved. Add the juices and whisk. Chill the mixture for 2 to 4 hours; it must be cold before going into the ice cream machine.

3. Pour the mixture into the machine's frozen canister and freeze according to the manufacturer's directions.

DRINKS

Our goals for the refreshments at True Food Kitchen are simple: Keep it natural; keep it refreshing. So our Honey Lemonade (page 220) is made from lemons, local honey, and water—it doesn't get more natural than that. We aim to keep our offerings up to date as well. As a response to "energy drinks" loaded with synthetics and sugars, we introduced the Medicine Man (page 221), which features antioxidant-rich superfoods including sea buckthorn juice, black tea for a gentle caffeinated lift, cranberry juice, and sparkling water. Our intention with the bar program is the same: We use organic liquors whenever possible; sweeten with agave, honey, or raw sugar; and source local fruits and vegetables for juices.

Our beverages—alcoholic or not—are all about balancing sweetness with acidity and flavor with nutrients, which is why it's essential that all ingredients be precisely measured. MS

Honey Lemonade

Honey is notoriously sticky and can be difficult to work with. When mixing, add the honey to the hot water before adding the lemon juice. This will make it easier to mix. Our recipe calls for equal parts of honey and lemon juice and approximately six parts of water. If you want to make a larger quantity, just follow the 1:1:6 ratio.

8   ounces honey

8   ounces freshly squeezed lemon juice

8   lemon wedges

Dissolve the honey in 6 cups hot water in a pitcher. Add the lemon juice and $2\frac{2}{3}$ cups cool water. Stir well and refrigerate until needed. Pour over ice into tall glasses and garnish each with a lemon wedge.

Green Arnie

Matcha is a finely ground Japanese green tea that requires proper mixing. The ratio for making the blend used here is 1 tablespoon matcha powder per 8 ounces of water. Look for matcha where quality teas are sold.

2   tablespoons matcha powder

64   ounces (8 cups) Honey Lemonade (see recipe at left)

8   lemon wedges

1. Pour the matcha into a bowl. Add $\frac{1}{4}$ cup hot water and whisk into a green paste. Slowly add $1\frac{3}{4}$ cups cool water and continue whisking until the color is uniform. The aroma will change from a dry and woodsy scent to an herbaceous scent. Refrigerate until needed; stir well before using.

2. Fill tall glasses with ice, pour in $\frac{1}{4}$ cup of the matcha blend, and fill each glass with the lemonade. Garnish with a lemon wedge.

Andy's Elixir

MAKES 1 SERVING

Totally simple and refreshing, this bright orange drink is a great way to experience the distinctive flavor of sea buckthorn fruit.

1   ounce sea buckthorn juice
1   ounce Simple Syrup (see page 242)
    Soda water

Put the sea buckthorn and Simple Syrup in a cocktail shaker. Shake well to combine. Fill a tall glass with ice cubes. Pour the sea buckthorn–agave blend into the glass. Fill the glass with soda water.

Medicine Man

MAKES 6 TO 8 SERVINGS

Here's one of our most popular beverages, full of fruit, rich in antioxidants, and with enough caffeine to provide a nice lift.

30 ounces (3¾ cups) unsweetened cranberry juice
20 ounces (2½ cups) strong brewed black tea, cooled
10 ounces (1¼ cups) unsweetened pomegranate juice
2½ ounces Simple Syrup (see page 242)
2½ ounces sea buckthorn juice
24 to 32 blueberries
    Soda water

1. Combine the cranberry juice, tea, pomegranate juice, Simple Syrup, and sea buckthorn juice in a pitcher. Refrigerate until needed.

2. Muddle 4 blueberries in each tall glass, then fill the glass two-thirds full with the tea-juice mixture. Stir to mix. Add ice cubes and fill the remainder of the glass with soda water. Serve with a straw.

A Better Berry

The best plants—like the best people—are often products of adversity, and this is especially true of the sea buckthorn, *Hippophae rhamnoides L.* A patch of land on which it seems nothing could grow is the perfect habitat for this indomitable shrub. From western Europe to northern China, it thrives in salt-sprayed beach sand, across the blistering deserts of central Asia, and above the frigid tree lines of many Eurasian mountain ranges.

And like many unstoppable people, the sea buckthorn's fruits can be off-putting at first. Abundant thorns surround its half-inch, orange-yellow spheres, and picking is so difficult that harvesters shake the whole bush and pluck berries from the ground. The taste of the berry is no friendlier—extremely acidic and oily. I first tried the juice in Italy—where it's known as *olivello*—when I visited the biodynamic farm of a Swiss grower who supplies the increasing demand for sea buckthorn for use in energy drinks and skin care products.

Sea buckthorn is one of the most nutritious, vitamin-packed fruits ever discovered, exceptionally high in antioxidants (vitamins C and E, carotenoids) and good fatty acids. This combination of nutrients has potent health-protective and therapeutic properties, which is why the oil extracts have long been used in Asia and Europe to lower inflammation, relieve pain, and promote tissue regeneration. Having found a reliable supply of high-quality, organically grown raw material, I was determined to make True Food Kitchen the first restaurant in the United States to offer sea buckthorn juice.

In the introduction to this book, I related how Michael invented Orange and Sea Buckthorn Sorbet (page 216), offsetting the juice's sour and astringent bite with the sweetness of orange juice and a mellowing vanilla note. We also use it in some of our most popular nonalcoholic drinks, such as Andy's Elixir (page 221) and Medicine Man (page 221). With the right companion ingredients, the juice is not just tolerable but actually delicious—deep, complex, and rewarding. AW

The Natural

A refreshing minimalist drink that marries fresh ginger and lime juices, this is delightful in warm weather.

1   (4-inch) piece fresh ginger, peeled and coarsely chopped

1   ounce Simple Syrup (see page 242)

½   ounce freshly squeezed lime juice

Soda water

1. Put the ginger in a blender with ½ cup hot water. Blend until the ginger is pulverized. Pour the contents through a fine-mesh strainer into a bowl, pressing on the pulp with a wooden spoon until all of the juices have been extracted. Refrigerate until needed (this makes enough for more than one drink).

2. Fill a tall glass with ice cubes and pour in 1 ounce of the ginger juice, Simple Syrup, and lime juice. Stir well and fill the glass with soda water.

Cucumber Refresher

Lemonade must be made with a sweetener, but some people find the result too one-dimensional to be truly refreshing. Adding cucumber juice introduces a vegetal note that cuts the sweetness and really helps slake a thirst. MS

1   cucumber, peeled, seeded, and diced

6   ounces (¾ cup) Honey Lemonade (page 220)

1   slice cucumber

1. If you don't have a juicer, put the cucumber in a blender with just enough water to blend. Blend until pureed, then strain the juice through a fine-mesh strainer into a bowl.

2. Fill a tall glass with ice cubes. Add the cucumber juice and lemonade and stir well. Garnish with the cucumber slice.

Lemon Sipper

MAKES 1 SERVING

My aim was simply to combine fresh, seasonal produce and high-quality spirits to make something as clean, bright, and tasty as possible. This classic summer cocktail quickly became one of our most popular drinks. MS

3 fresh mint leaves

4 ounces (½ cup) Honey Lemonade (page 220)

1½ ounces vodka

1 lemon twist

Put the mint and 1 ounce of the Honey Lemonade in a cocktail shaker and muddle the mint. Add the vodka and remaining 3 ounces lemonade, along with some ice cubes. Shake vigorously. Pour the contents of the shaker into a tall glass and garnish with the lemon twist.

Peacemaker

MAKES 1 SERVING

The Peacemaker features a black tea syrup, rye whiskey, and Averna, an Italian digestivo. *Be sure to shake the cocktail vigorously.*

1 tablespoon honey

1 ounce strong brewed black tea, cooled

½ ounce freshly squeezed lemon juice

1½ ounces rye whiskey

¼ ounce Averna liqueur

2 lemon twists

Combine the honey, tea, and lemon juice in a cocktail shaker. Add the whiskey, Averna, and some ice cubes and shake well. Pour the contents of the shaker into a tall glass. Garnish with the lemon twists.

Tamarind Margarita

MAKES 1 SERVING

Tamarind paste (available at Indian food stores and online) has a rich, raisin-like aroma and a pureed-fig texture, and it keeps for months in your pantry. It is mixed with agave and a little bit of hot water to make a tamarind syrup for this cocktail.

TAMARIND-AGAVE SYRUP
Makes about 1 cup

5   ounces agave nectar

1   ounce tamarind paste

1. Put the agave nectar and tamarind paste in a lidded jar along with 1 ounce hot water, and shake well to combine. Store in the refrigerator.

MARGARITA

1½ ounces silver tequila

½   ounce orange liqueur, such as Cointreau

1½ ounces freshly squeezed lime juice

1   lime slice

2. Combine the tequila, orange liqueur, 1½ ounces of the Tamarind-Agave Syrup, and lime juice in a cocktail shaker. Fill the shaker with ice cubes and shake vigorously. Strain into a stemmed glass and garnish with the lime slice.

Shiso Spirit

MAKES 1 SERVING

For this drink, you'll need a variety of Asian ingredients: dry sake, yuzu, and shiso leaves. Use a dry premium sake, such as a Junmai Ginjo variety, available at liquor stores and online.

2   fresh shiso or mint leaves

1   ounce Simple Syrup (page 242)

½   ounce yuzu juice

2   lemon wedges

1½ ounces rye whiskey

1   ounce dry sake

Put 1 shiso leaf, Simple Syrup, yuzu juice, and lemon wedges in a cocktail shaker and muddle. Add the whiskey, sake, and some ice cubes. Shake lightly. Strain into a glass filled with fresh ice and garnish with the remaining shiso leaf.

Weil-y Coyote

MAKES 1 SERVING

We like clementine oranges in this cocktail, but you may use any orange in season. Tombo Shochu, sold at liquor stores, is a Japanese distilled spirit made from barley, rice, or sweet potatoes. It is stronger than sake but weaker than whiskey or vodka.

- 3 **clementine segments**
- 3 **ounces Simple Syrup (page 242)**
- ½ **ounce yuzu juice**
- 2 **ounces Tombo Shochu**

Put the clementine segments, Simple Syrup, and yuzu juice in a cocktail shaker and muddle. Add the Tombo Shochu and ice cubes. Shake vigorously and then pour everything into a glass.

Açai Mojito

Weil-y Coyote

Shiso Spirit

Açai Mojito

MAKES 1 SERVING

Look for VeeV açai liqueur in well-stocked liquor stores. As with the classic and traditional mojito, mint, citrus, white rum, and simple syrup work together to balance the sweet, sharp, and tart tastes.

6   blueberries

5   fresh mint leaves

3/4   ounce freshly squeezed lemon juice

3/4   ounce Simple Syrup (page 242)

1   ounce white rum

1   ounce VeeV açai liqueur

   Soda water

1   sprig mint

Combine 5 of the blueberries, mint leaves, lemon juice, and Simple Syrup in a cocktail shaker and muddle. Add the rum and açai liqueur. Add ice cubes and shake vigorously. Strain into a tall glass filled partway with ice. Add soda water to fill the glass. Garnish with the remaining blueberry and the mint sprig.

Cucumber-Kumquat Skinny

MAKES 1 SERVING

This cocktail is a light blend of mint and cucumber, which are classic cocktail mates, and a seasonal citrus—kumquat.

3/4   ounce Simple Syrup (page 242)

1/2   ounce freshly squeezed lime juice

5   fresh mint leaves

1   kumquat, cut into wedges

4   cucumber rounds

1 1/2   ounces silver tequila

3/4   ounce triple sec

   Soda water

Put the Simple Syrup, lime juice, mint leaves, kumquat, and cucumber rounds in a cocktail shaker and muddle. Add the tequila, triple sec, and some ice cubes. Shake vigorously. Strain into a tall glass filled with ice. Top with soda water.

Pomegranate Martini

This tart and racy cocktail is a nod to both Prohibition-era gin cocktails and millennium-themed martinis. Pama is a pomegranate-flavored liqueur.

2   lemon wedges

10 blueberries

1   ounce unsweetened pomegranate juice

1½ ounces gin

1   ounce maraschino cherry liqueur

½   ounce Pama liqueur

Put the lemon wedges, blueberries, and pomegranate juice in a cocktail shaker and muddle together. Add the gin, cherry liqueur, and Pama, along with some ice cubes. Shake well. Strain into a martini glass.

Prana

If making this cocktail for a large group of people, combine the juices ahead to save time.

3   clementine segments

1   lemon wedge

1   ounce pineapple juice

1½ ounces vodka

1   ounce coconut water

1   ounce grapefruit juice

1   grapefruit segment

Put the clementine segments, lemon wedge, and pineapple juice in a cocktail shaker and muddle. Add the vodka, coconut water, and grapefruit juice. Shake vigorously. Strain into a martini glass. Garnish with the grapefruit segment.

BASICS

Each of these recipes, used in many of the other recipes in this book, provides fundamental flavors to True Food. Many of the dressings, sauces, and condiments can be swapped or combined when cooking. Experiment with your own creations. Having these basics on hand will boost the flavors in all your cooking.

Unless otherwise noted, these basics will keep for a week in the refrigerator. The stocks may be portioned into airtight containers and frozen until ready to use.

Balsamic Vinaigrette

MAKES 1¼ CUPS

This is a basic dressing, good on cooked vegetables and grilled fish as well as green salads. Use a high-quality balsamic vinegar that has some body to it. If you like garlic in your vinaigrette, add a mashed clove to the vinegar, salt, and pepper in the blender.

- ⅓ **cup balsamic vinegar**
- ¼ **teaspoon salt**
- ⅛ **teaspoon freshly ground black pepper**
- ⅔ **cup extra-virgin olive oil**

Put the vinegar, salt, and pepper in a food processor or blender. Pulse to combine the ingredients. With the machine running, slowly drizzle in the oil and blend until the dressing is emulsified. Pour into a lidded container and refrigerate until ready to use. Shake well before using.

Champagne Vinaigrette

MAKES 1 CUP

Champagne vinegar, made from Champagne grapes (which are actually Black Corinth grapes and not the grapes used to make Champagne), is lighter and more complex than other vinegars.

- ¼ **cup champagne vinegar**
- 1 **tablespoon honey**
- ¼ **teaspoon salt**
  Pinch freshly ground black pepper
- ¾ **cup expeller-pressed canola oil**

Put the vinegar, honey, salt, and pepper in a blender. Pulse to combine the ingredients. With the machine running, drizzle in the canola oil. Blend the dressing until it is well emulsified and thick. Pour into a lidded container and refrigerate until ready to use. Shake well before using.

Carrot-Miso Vinaigrette

MAKES ABOUT 1 CUP

If you've ordered green salads in Japanese restaurants, they have probably been topped with a version of this thick, brightly colored, highly flavored dressing. It makes a welcome change from familiar vinaigrettes.

2   medium carrots, coarsely chopped
2   tablespoons expeller-pressed canola oil
¼   cup unseasoned rice wine vinegar
3   tablespoons white (*shiro*) miso
1   (1-inch) piece ginger, peeled and grated
2   teaspoons evaporated cane sugar
½   teaspoon salt
½   teaspoon freshly ground black pepper

Put the carrots and 1 tablespoon of the oil in a food processor or blender. Pulse and blend until the carrots are ground into very small pieces. Add all of the remaining ingredients, plus 1 tablespoon water, and blend until emulsified. The dressing will be thick. If too thick, add another tablespoon of water and blend to the desired consistency. Pour into a lidded container and refrigerate until ready to use. Shake well before using.

Vegetarian Caesar Dressing

MAKES 2¾ CUPS

Suitable for lacto-vegetarians, this dressing omits egg yolk, substitutes Kalamata olives for anchovies, and uses vegetarian Worcestershire sauce (available in natural foods stores) instead of the usual anchovy-based version. Many people say they prefer this version to the classic recipe.

½   cup freshly squeezed lemon juice
2   tablespoons red wine vinegar
1   tablespoon vegetarian Worcestershire sauce
¼   scant cup Dijon mustard
½   cup pitted Kalamata olives
6   garlic cloves, chopped
1   cup grated packed Parmigiano-Reggiano cheese
2   cups extra-virgin olive oil
1½ teaspoons salt (or more to taste)
1   teaspoon freshly ground black pepper (or more to taste)

Combine the lemon juice, vinegar, Worcestershire, mustard, olives, garlic, and cheese in a blender or food processor. Blend to a smooth paste. With the machine on, drizzle in the oil, salt, and pepper. Blend until thick and emulsified, like mayonnaise. Adjust the seasonings with salt and pepper. Transfer to a lidded jar and refrigerate for up to 3 days.

Kale Pesto

MAKES 2 CUPS

The word pesto *comes from an Italian word meaning "to pound or crush." Although pesto made with basil is best known, it can be prepared with a variety of greens and herbs. Freeze any extra in ice cube trays and use the cubes in soups or when making tomato sauce.*

8   cups stemmed chopped black kale (about 2 bunches)

1   cup grated Parmigiano-Reggiano cheese

¾   cup extra-virgin olive oil

½   cup pine nuts

4   garlic cloves, chopped

2   teaspoons salt

½   teaspoon red pepper flakes

1.   Bring a large pot of water to a boil. Fill a large bowl with ice cubes and cold water.

2.   Plunge the kale into the boiling water for 3 minutes. Using tongs or a slotted spoon, transfer the kale from the hot water to the ice bath. The cold water allows the kale to keep its bright green color. After 3 minutes, drain the kale in a colander, then squeeze it firmly to press out excess water.

3.   Put the kale and all of the remaining ingredients in a food processor and puree until smooth. Transfer to a container, cover, and refrigerate until ready to use. The pesto will keep for up to 3 days.

Asian Barbecue Sauce

MAKES 1¼ CUPS

Keep a container of this tangy sauce in the refrigerator and brush it on chicken, shrimp, or vegetables before grilling.

½   cup ketchup

2   tablespoons low-sodium soy sauce

2   tablespoons red wine vinegar

2   tablespoons honey mustard

1   tablespoon dark brown sugar

2   teaspoons curry powder

1   teaspoon ground cumin

1   teaspoon hot sauce

½   teaspoon salt

¼   cup chopped fresh cilantro

Combine the ketchup, soy sauce, vinegar, mustard, brown sugar, curry powder, cumin, hot sauce, and salt in a bowl and whisk to combine. Stir in the cilantro. Transfer the sauce to a lidded container and refrigerate until ready to use.

Citrus-Sesame Sauce

MAKES 1 CUP

A wok sauce, designed to be added while cooking, needs to bloom in high heat, and this one does. Lighter in color and far less salty than most, it features plenty of both acidity and savory depth. The real cross-cultural innovation here is tahini, rare in Asian cooking, which ably thickens the sauce and provides a creamy note to balance the lemony tang. Very versatile, this will work wonders with any green veggie, as well as with chicken or shrimp.

½   cup tahini

⅓   cup freshly squeezed
     lemon juice

2   tablespoons low-sodium
     soy sauce

1   tablespoon dark
     sesame oil

1   tablespoon grated
     fresh ginger

1   tablespoon evaporated
     cane sugar

2   teaspoons freshly grated
     lemon zest

2   teaspoons toasted
     sesame seeds

1   teaspoon salt

Whisk all of the ingredients together in a bowl. Transfer to a lidded container and refrigerate until ready to use. Stir well before using.

Teriyaki Sauce

MAKES 2 CUPS

This is a cleaned-up version of an old standby, light enough to let the fresh fruit flavors shine through. Pectins in the fruit thicken the sauce naturally.

¾   cup chopped fresh pineapple

1   Fuji, Gala, or Honeycrisp apple,
     cored and cut into wedges

1   tablespoon chopped fresh ginger

1   scallion, cut into 1-inch pieces

½   cup packed light brown sugar

⅓   cup freshly squeezed orange juice

⅓   cup low-sodium soy sauce

1. Combine all of the ingredients in a saucepan over medium heat. Bring to a simmer and then reduce the heat to low. Continue to cook for 20 minutes, until the fruit is soft.

2. Allow the mixture to cool for 20 minutes, then transfer to a blender or use an immersion blender to puree. Hold the lid down firmly with a clean, folded towel over it. Start on low speed and blend until it is a smooth sauce. Transfer to a lidded container and refrigerate for up to 3 days. Stir well before using.

Tomato Sauce

MAKES 3 CUPS

San Marzano tomatoes from Italy are the best canned tomatoes for cooking. Feel free to double the recipe and keep it on hand to make pasta dishes, soups, and stews.

1	tablespoon extra-virgin olive oil
3	garlic cloves, minced
1	(28-ounce) can San Marzano tomatoes, chopped, with juice
1	teaspoon salt
¼	teaspoon ground allspice
	Pinch of freshly ground black pepper
2	tablespoons chopped fresh basil
1	tablespoon chopped fresh oregano leaves

1. Heat the oil in a saucepan over medium heat. Add the garlic, reduce the heat to low, and cook for 2 minutes, stirring constantly. Add the tomatoes, salt, allspice, pepper, basil, and oregano. Bring to a simmer, and simmer for 20 minutes.

2. Allow the sauce to cool for 20 minutes, then transfer to a blender. Hold the lid down firmly with a clean, folded towel over it. Start on low speed and blend until it is a smooth sauce. Transfer to a lidded container and refrigerate for up to 5 days, or freeze for up to 3 months.

Umami Sauce

MAKES 1½ CUPS

This novel, intriguing sauce is so simple to make. Most people cannot guess the ingredients, particularly the nutritional yeast flakes that give the sauce its rich ocher color and clear fifth taste (umami). I keep a jar of it in my refrigerator and use it on everything from steamed vegetables to broiled fish. It's great on salads, but add it at the last minute and don't toss it with delicate greens, lest it wilt.

¼	cup apple cider vinegar
3	tablespoons tamari
¼	cup water
1	cup nutritional yeast flakes
8	garlic cloves, mashed
½	cup extra-virgin olive oil
	Salt (optional)

Put the vinegar, tamari, water, yeast flakes, and garlic in a blender or food processor and blend until well combined. Remove the feed tube and, with the machine running, slowly drizzle in the olive oil. Blend well until the mixture becomes thick and emulsified, like mayonnaise. Adjust the seasoning with salt as needed. Pour the mixture into a lidded jar and refrigerate for up to 2 weeks. Bring the sauce to room temperature and shake well before using.

Wok Aromatics

We use these aromatics in our Asian-inspired dishes to add flavor, complexity, and spiciness. They may also be added to marinades and even dressings to give them an Asian kick. It is important to slice the ginger and lemongrass across the fibrous stalks; otherwise the mixture will become stringy when blended. Freeze any leftover Wok Aromatics, since the flavors dissipate if not used immediately.

1   lemongrass stalk, thinly sliced
     (about ⅓ cup)

⅓   cup thinly sliced fresh ginger

5 or 6 scallions, white part only,
     coarsely chopped

1½ teaspoons sambal oelek

Combine the lemongrass, ginger, and scallions in a food processor and pulse until finely minced. Transfer the mixture to a lidded jar, add the sambal oelek, and mix well to combine. Use immediately, and freeze any left over.

Chicken Stock

Toss all those extra chicken wings, backs, and necks into a plastic bag in the freezer and, when you have a pound or more, make chicken stock. Divide the cooked and cooled stock among plastic containers or ice cube trays and freeze. You'll have stock on hand whenever you need it. This may seem like a lot of chicken stock, but as it simmers, the stock reduces.

1   pound chicken bones

2   celery stalks, cut into
     large pieces

2   carrots, cut into large pieces

1   onion, quartered

2   garlic cloves, mashed

8   sprigs thyme

15 black peppercorns

1. Put the chicken in a large pot and add 4 to 5 quarts cold water to cover. Bring to a simmer over medium-high heat and skim off any foam from the surface. Add the celery, carrots, onion, garlic, thyme, and peppercorns. Let the stock simmer for 2 hours, partially covered.

2. Strain the stock through a fine-mesh strainer, discard the solids, and let cool in the refrigerator. Store in lidded containers in the refrigerator for up to 3 days, or freeze for up to 3 months.

Mushroom Stock

MAKES 2 QUARTS

Stock used in restaurants is usually made with chicken, but we serve so many vegetarian dishes that we needed something different for our sauces and soups. Shiitake mushrooms impart a savory essence; you'll never miss the meat. Make it in volume; it keeps for a week in the refrigerator or a month in the freezer.

2   celery stalks, chopped

1   medium onion, chopped

2   ounces dried shiitake mushrooms

½   cup low-sodium soy sauce

1. Put the celery, onion, mushrooms, and 2½ quarts water into a large pot. Bring to a simmer over medium-high heat, then reduce the heat and let the stock cook for 20 minutes.

2. Turn off the heat, cover, and let the stock steep for 20 minutes. Add the soy sauce. Strain the stock through a fine-mesh strainer, discard the solids, and let cool. Use as needed, or put into lidded containers and refrigerate for up to 1 week or freeze for up to 1 month.

Dashi

MAKES 7 TO 8 CUPS

This mushroom-seaweed Japanese stock is used in many dishes. You can find dried shiitakes, kombu, and bonito flakes in Asian and other markets.

2   quarts Mushroom Stock (see recipe at left)

2   ounces dried shiitake mushroom caps

1   (20-inch square) piece kombu

½   cup bonito flakes

1   tablespoon evaporated cane sugar

¼   cup low-sodium soy sauce

1. Put the Mushroom Stock, shiitakes, and kombu in a large pot and bring to a boil. Cook over medium heat for 20 minutes, skimming off foam as necessary. Remove the kombu. Reduce the heat to a simmer and cook for 45 minutes.

2. Remove from the heat and whisk in the bonito flakes and sugar. Let the stock cool for 20 minutes. Strain through a fine-mesh strainer and discard the solids. Stir in the soy sauce. Transfer to lidded containers and refrigerate for up to 3 days, or freeze for up to 1 month.

Cashew Milk

MAKES 3 CUPS

A tasty vegan alternative to cow's milk, with a healthier fatty acid profile than coconut milk, this is good in both sweet and savory dishes. Make leaner or richer versions by varying the proportion of nuts to water.

1   **cup raw cashews, whole or pieces**

1. Grind the cashews to a fine powder in a blender or food processor, stopping and stirring occasionally to ensure uniform grinding. Depending on the machine you use, this will take 1 to 3 minutes. Stop before the nuts turn into a paste.

2. Add 2 cups room temperature water, blend on medium speed for 30 seconds, and then stop and stir up any nuts that stick to the sides of the container. Blend on high speed for 2 minutes. Store in the refrigerator for up to 5 days. Shake well before using.

Annatto Oil

MAKES ½ CUP

Annatto, from the fruit pulp and seeds of the tropical achiote tree, is virtually tasteless in small quantities. Its principal virtue is its ability to impart a rich golden orange hue to foods, such as butter and cheddar cheese. Seeds are available in specialty food stores or online. If tracking them down is too daunting, a pinch of turmeric can accomplish something similar.

½   **cup extra-virgin olive oil**
1   **tablespoon annatto seeds**

Heat the oil and annatto seeds in a small saucepan over low heat until the oil is bright orange-red and aromatic, about 10 minutes. Take care not to overheat the oil. Strain out the seeds and let the oil cool. If not using immediately, store in a lidded container in the refrigerator for up to 2 weeks.

Oven-Roasted Tomatoes

MAKES 2 CUPS

When it's tomato season, double or triple this recipe and keep this condiment on hand to add to salads, sandwiches, or pastas. We like an array of different, colorful tomatoes—from large ones and heirlooms to grape and cherry— but if you can only find red ones, that's fine.

- 4   red tomatoes, halved
- 4   orange tomatoes, halved
- 4   yellow tomatoes, halved
- ½   teaspoon salt
- ¼   teaspoon freshly ground black pepper
- 6   sprigs oregano
- 12   sprigs thyme
- 3   tablespoons extra-virgin olive oil

1. Preheat the oven to 200°F. Line two baking sheets with silicone baking mats or aluminum foil.

2. Arrange the tomatoes in a single layer on the prepared pans, cut sides up. Season the tomatoes with the salt and pepper. Lay the herb sprigs on the tomatoes and drizzle everything with the oil. Bake for 2 hours, until wrinkled but still juicy.

3. Let cool on a wire rack. Remove and discard the herbs and tomato skins and transfer the roasted tomatoes to a lidded container. Refrigerate until ready to use, or freeze for up to 6 months.

Caramelized Onions

MAKES 2 CUPS

When slowly cooked over low heat, thinly sliced onions become sweet and meltingly tender. This may seem like a lot of onions, but when cooked, the amount shrinks significantly. Keep a batch of these onions on hand to use as a pasta or burger topping, combine with nonfat plain yogurt to make onion dip, or use as a flavor booster in soups.

- 1   tablespoon expeller-pressed canola oil
- 3   large onions, thinly sliced

Heat the canola oil in a large nonstick skillet over low heat. Add the onions and cook for 30 minutes, stirring often, until they are soft and brown. Let cool, and then store in a lidded container in the refrigerator for up to 3 days.

Pickled Cucumbers

MAKES ABOUT 2 CUPS

You may use any variety of cucumbers—Kirby, Persian, English—to make these pickles. Keep a batch on hand and serve with sandwiches, burgers, or salads. If you have a mandoline, use it to get the thinnest cucumber slices possible.

1½ cups unseasoned rice
   wine vinegar

1   cup evaporated cane sugar

2   teaspoons salt

2 to 4 cucumbers, depending on
   variety, thinly sliced

Combine the vinegar, sugar, and salt in a saucepan. Place over medium-high heat and simmer until the sugar and salt dissolve. Put the cucumbers in a bowl, cover with the vinegar mixture, and let sit for 2 hours. Drain the cucumbers, and store in a lidded container in the refrigerator for up to 1 week.

Pickled Red Onions

MAKES ABOUT 2 CUPS

Here's another easy-to-make pickle to keep on hand, especially for chicken, turkey, or salmon burgers. Add a few red pepper flakes for a little heat.

1½ cups unseasoned rice
   wine vinegar

1   cup evaporated cane sugar

2   teaspoons salt

2   medium red onions, thinly sliced

Combine the vinegar, sugar, and salt in a saucepan. Place over medium-high heat and simmer until the sugar and salt dissolve. Put the onions in a bowl, cover with the vinegar mixture, and let sit for at least 30 minutes. Drain the onions, and store in a lidded container in the refrigerator for up to 1 week.

Roasted Mushrooms

When roasted rather than sautéed, mushrooms retain their moisture and become lightly caramelized. Although three different types of mushrooms are suggested below, you may substitute any variety in any amount. Use as a topping on pasta or bison burgers. Save the shiitake stems to use in stock or soup.

8   ounces shiitake mushrooms, stemmed and thinly sliced

6   ounces oyster mushrooms, thinly sliced

4   ounces maitake mushrooms, torn into small pieces

3   tablespoons extra-virgin olive oil

½   teaspoon salt

     Pinch of freshly ground black pepper

1. Preheat the oven to 400°F. Line a baking sheet with a silicone baking mat or parchment paper.

2. Toss together all of the mushrooms in a large bowl. Add the oil, salt, and pepper, tossing to coat the mushrooms. Arrange the seasoned mushrooms in a single layer on the prepared baking sheet. Bake for 12 to 15 minutes, until soft, lightly browned, and beginning to become crisp. When cool, transfer to a lidded container and store in the refrigerator for up to 3 days.

Simple Syrup

This is the most neutral liquid sweetener possible. As with all sweeteners, use it sparingly.

1   cup evaporated cane sugar

Combine the evaporated cane sugar and 1 cup water in a saucepan over medium heat. Heat and stir until the sugar dissolves. Let cool, then put it in a lidded jar and refrigerate until needed.

Toasted Nuts

Because they have high oil content and continue to cook after being removed from the heat source, nuts can quickly turn from perfectly toasted to burned. A general rule is that once you can smell the nuts, they are done.

1. To toast nuts on the stovetop: Spread a single layer of nuts in a dry skillet and set over medium heat. Move the nuts around the pan, turning them over, every minute or two. When you can smell the nuts and they begin to color, transfer them to a plate to cool.

2. To toast nuts in the oven: Preheat the oven to 350°F. Spread a single layer of nuts on a baking sheet and bake for 10 to 15 minutes.

3. Toasted nuts quickly go rancid, so use them up soon after preparing them.

Index

Page numbers in *italic* refer to photographs.

Acknowledgments

A number of people helped us compile this book. We are grateful to our literary agent, Richard Pine, and to Richard Baxter of Weil Lifestyle, who worked together to make this book a reality. We give big thanks to the people who worked on the project at Little, Brown and Company: our editor, Tracy Behar, publisher Michael Pietsch, and art director Mario Pulice.

Brad Lemley, editorial director of Weil Lifestyle, LLC, conducted interviews, gathered needed information, and provided editorial assistance, as did Chris Willett.

Deborah Knight worked with Michael to develop and test recipes. In his words, "Her encyclopedic knowledge of ingredients helped the process immensely; she made it easy for me every day." Michael also thanks his wife, Ally, for her support.

Harriet Bell reviewed all the recipes, making sure they were written correctly for the home cook.

It was a joy to work with Ditte Isager. Her outstanding photographs capture the essence of True Food Kitchen.

All of us are indebted to the ever-growing True Food family, including the chefs and managers and especially Mike Wilcox, Clint Woods, Christopher Cristiano, Regan Jasper, and Matt Snapp.

Finally, we deeply appreciate the loyalty of all those who enjoy the food we serve and who have made True Food Kitchen so successful.

About the Authors

Andrew Weil, MD, is a world-renowned leader and pioneer in the field of integrative medicine, a healing-oriented approach to health care that encompasses body, mind, and spirit.

Dr. Weil is the founder and director of the Arizona Center for Integrative Medicine at the University of Arizona Health Sciences Center, where he is also a clinical professor of medicine, professor of public health, and the Lovell-Jones Professor of Integrative Rheumatology. Dr. Weil received both his medical degree and his undergraduate degree in biology (botany) from Harvard University.

Dr. Weil is an internationally recognized expert on maintaining a healthy lifestyle, healthy aging, and the future of medicine and health care. Approximately 10 million copies of Dr. Weil's books have been sold, including *Spontaneous Happiness, Spontaneous Healing, 8 Weeks to Optimum Health, Eating Well for Optimum Health, The Healthy Kitchen,* and *Healthy Aging.*

He is the editorial director of drweil.com, the leading online resource for healthy living based on the philosophy of integrative medicine. He authors the popular "Self-Healing" special publications and is Director of Integrative Health and Healing at Miraval Resort in Tucson, Arizona. As a columnist for *Prevention* magazine and frequent guest on numerous national shows, Dr. Weil provides valuable insight and information on how to incorporate conventional and complementary medicine practices into one's life to optimize the body's natural healing power.

Sam Fox is one of the nation's most successful restaurateurs and the CEO of Fox Restaurant Concepts. His vision has led to the development of 12 unique restaurant concepts that have now grown into 31 restaurants in Arizona, California, Colorado, Kansas, and Texas. For the past three years, Fox has been nominated as Restaurateur of the Year by the prestigious James Beard Foundation. A highly sought-after speaker, he is also a member of the Young President's Organization and the philanthropic Thunderbirds. In addition, he serves on the Board of the Arizona Cancer Center, the Scottsdale Convention and Visitors Bureau Tourism Development Commission, and several other organizations. He lives in Scottsdale, Arizona.

Michael Stebner is an award-winning chef and the executive chef of True Food Kitchen. He was previously the head of the culinary team at the Greene House restaurant in Scottsdale, Arizona, and the owner and operator of Region, a restaurant in San Diego, California, which was named in *Gourmet* magazine's "Where to Eat Right Now in 30 American Cities" list. He has also worked in the kitchens of Azzura Point at the Loews Coronado Bay Resort, Caesar's Palace in Las Vegas, the French Laundry in Yountville, California, and others. Stebner has twice been invited to the renowned James Beard House in New York City and has served as one of only two San Diego delegates at Slow Food's biannual convention in Italy. He lives in Scottsdale, Arizona.